The JUMP *into* LIFE
MOVING BEYOND FEAR

by Arnaud Desjardins

HOHM PRESS

Hohm Press, P.O. Box 2501, Prescott, Arizona, U.S.A. 86302

First English Edition Published 1994
Printed in the United States of America

Original edition published by EDITIONS DE LA TABLE RONDE 1989
FRANCE under the title of *L'Audace de Vivre* by Arnaud Desjardins

English translation by Kathleen Kennedy.

Library of Congress No. 93-080524
ISBN 0-934252-42-4

TABLE OF CONTENTS

FOREWORD

I HAVE met Arnaud Desjardins on only a few occasions, each quite pleasant, but I cannot claim to know him well. Yet, I am pleased to endorse him and this book, which is the direct expression of this teaching, because of little things that have occurred during and after our visits. Once I received a letter from him of thanks (for circumstances that are not relevant to discuss here). The simple openness and gladness expressed in that letter bore eloquent testimony to a man who is above all else a fine person with a generous heart.

As one reads *The Jump Into Life*, the fineness of the author breathes between the words like a sure but gentle nectar. One senses a prayer of compassion for the real suffering of life, and gratitude for the wonder of life. There is love in these words and precious and timeless wisdom. In the West in particular, there are few whom we can call spiritual elders, especially those who have taken the unique point of view and wisdom of the East and embodied it authentically and relevantly in a western life and teaching. Arnaud Desjardins is such a person. There are thousands of days of real experience with people underlying the thoughts, images and teaching that emerge in *The Jump Into Life*. In this day and age when "enlightenment" is sold in weekend seminars and "masters" can be trained in a few months, the wealth of a lifetime of search and decades of direct teaching with people from every walk of life is precious. Indeed, it is irreplaceable.

I am not saying I agree with everything Arnaud has said, nor would I expect the reader to. Deep truths can only be comprehended from many points of view, and while each such point of view may be true in itself, side by side they can appear contradictory. The important thing is the contrasts that complement our own vision and experience and help us to see more completely. Even on the very few occasions when my mind hesitated, considering an alternative point of view, my heart knew that it was in the presence of depth that went beyond and reconciled any seeming polarity hidden in the thoughts. For example, in the remarks about the sex center, I could not help but think that the "yes" or "no" a woman might express might have a fundamentally different basis than a man's. In particular, I suspect a woman might have a deep "no" at the sexual level that is not merely neurotic "contamination" from negative emotional or mental forces. The miracle and enormous consequences to her of pregnancy, childbirth and child-rearing might make both her "yes" and her "no" far more discerning than any man might imagine. But then we need more women of the equivalent depth and experience of someone such as Arnaud Desjardins to speak to these deep issues from their living truth. In the meantime, we can be grateful that a person such as Arnaud Desjardins is alive and calling us each to a fuller and more authentic life.

—*Richard Moss*
September 1993

INTRODUCTION

Lɪᴋᴇ others before it, this book has been compiled from answers to questions I have been asked and from recorded talks. It was born from the doubts, sufferings and inhibitions of those I was speaking to and therefore keeps the familiar tone one uses when addressing another directly and personally. Veronique Loiseleur has helped a great deal in choosing, compiling and restructuring the content of these talks. *The Jump Into Life*, in its present form, owes much to her.

Ever since people have started reading my books, I have received two totally contradictory kinds of critique. There are those who accuse me of extolling the virtues of Hinduism and Buddhism while greatly underestimating God's revelation to the prophets and His becoming man through Jesus Christ. These people consider me a propagandist of Oriental religions, who confuses Christians; in particular, they see me as someone who turns young people away from the Church. Then there are those who condemn the references I make to the Gospels as well as the religious language I sometimes use, seeing these as proof of Arnaud Desjardins' flagrant misunderstanding of Vedantic non-dualism. The latter go so far as to consider this a betrayal of my own guru, Swami Prajnanpad. It is true that out of the approximately 300 interviews that Swamiji gave me over a period of nine years, only once did he refer to God as a Father. He used strictly non-dualistic terms in which there was no mention of a personal God. Yet one of the last things he said to me was: "You can follow Swamiji, Arnaud, but you cannot imitate

Swamiji." For me, following Swamiji means taking into account the needs of those who address themselves to me and using whatever language it is that they can understand, not only with their minds but also with their hearts. At the same time, I make no secret of my belief that religious paths and the Yoga of Knowledge both lead to the same inner freedom, the same universal love. Ramdas, whose name means "slave of God," was as much a sage in my eyes as was Ramana Maharshi – although the latter recommended above all the direct search for the Self.

At various times in this book, you will find references to two men who taught in the West: Karlfried von Dürkheim (who left us in December, 1988) and G.I. Gurdjieff. I cannot submit these pages without expressing my gratitude toward each of these men who outwardly appeared to be so different from each other.

—*Arnaud Desjardins*

Note: So that each chapter will be complete in itself, we have
retained certain repetitions found in the original talks.

1

DARE TO LIVE

ONE day, as I was answering a question on the subject of death, the following words came to me: "You are not afraid of death, you are afraid of life." Thinking over that response, I realized how true it was. Our fear of death is all the greater when we have not dared to live. In fact, if you stop fearing life, you can no longer fear death because you will have discovered within yourself what Life really is. (Not your own life, but the unique and universal Life that nourishes us.) And it becomes obvious that such life is independent of birth and death.

Westerners commonly consider life to be the opposite of death, but Orientals consider birth to be the opposite of death. For them, life expresses itself through a movement of perpetual change: an uninterrupted play of death and birth. Many spiritual paths share this conviction. My own "guru," Swami Prajnanpad, gave simple examples to illustrate this: the birth of the child is the death of the baby; the birth of the adolescent is the death of the child.

Daring to live means daring to die at each moment. But it also means daring to be born – daring to pass through important stages in life where the person you used to be dies, in order to make room for someone with a new view of the world (assuming that there are various levels before the ultimate level of Awakening). It is a case of being more and more aware that each moment you are born and you die . . . you die and you are reborn.

To put it simply, daring to live also means no longer having the slightest fear of what we feel. I am sure that many of you agree with me, especially those who have begun to discover what lies within their own unconscious. You are afraid of what you bear inside because you cannot fully count on yourself; you know from experience that you tend to get yourself into situations which you end up bitterly regretting. But you are also afraid of what you carry inside because each of you, as a child, has experienced situations where the way you expressed yourself was brutally contradicted. Your joy of living, high spirits or fervor led to catastrophe when you found yourself being severely reprimanded for something you had been so happily doing.

Perhaps through therapy you had the chance to re-experience how bewildered you were to see your parents overcome with anger, when you had been having so much fun cutting up the best curtains in the house with a big pair of scissors. I once used the shoes of everyone in my family for boats in the bathtub. My parents didn't have much money at the time and there weren't very many shoes in the closet, but there were enough for me to float. Although that sounds quite harmless, it was an incident I re-experienced with tragic intensity, between my mother's despair, my father's severity and my own shattered happiness. I couldn't understand why something that had been such fun had upset my mother so much. She was convinced that all the shoes in the house were completely ruined.

It often turns out that something which was a small incident in the eyes of the parents was actually a terrible event in the eyes of the child we once were. A fear of what we are capable of very quickly takes hold of us. From then on, unless our parents are particularly careful, we ourselves start to smother our own life force. We start repressing our vital impulses. Then, as both psychology and self-observation show us, our discovery of the sexual world often takes place in an atmosphere of uneasiness, misunderstanding and a certain guilt that accompanies childish masturbation. The urges which arise in us during adolescence, which cannot always be satisfied as we would wish, leave us troubled and lost. We no longer completely accept the very powerful life force or libido within us. Hence, in a world of increasingly free moral standards, where there are enormous possibilities for self-expression and many opportunities to travel, the majority of you no longer dare to live fully. And once you no longer completely assume the life force within you, you begin to fear death. But the fear of death is an illusion; do not be bothered by the fear of dying. What is really important is to free yourself from the fear to live.

There are two faces to this fear of living: one is the fear of what is inside us; the other is the fear of concrete situations and of the consequences they can bring about. Very quickly, our fear of living turns into a fear of suffering. We feel that it is better to live less, so as to suffer less. Look inside yourself; see what is there; ask yourself if this is how you feel. Private interviews and group meetings with those who come here to our center have shown me how true this is. You are afraid to live because to live means to take the risk of suffering. This fear is rooted in past experience which showed you that the more you lived, the more unhappy you became. Not only because your enthusiasm may have led you to put shoes into the bathtub but because when you fell in love at the age of eighteen, you ended up suffering so much. Consequently, a certain decision tends to surge up inside – sometimes unconsciously, sometimes quite consciously – "I don't want to suffer like that any more." Now that is a very fine decision to make . . . but it leads to another one which is totally false, "so I will never love again" or "so I will never put myself into dangerous situations again." The fact is you must realize that if you commit yourself to the path of knowledge, if you want to gradually pierce the secret of suffering, it is essential to take the risk of living and of suffering.

Your childhood vitality and perhaps even your exuberance often brought about rebuke. You heard statements like, "You shouldn't do that!" or "How dare you do that!" And so this vitality or exuberance became associated with value judgements. Spiritual teachings also seem to greatly condemn the richness of life; they recommend asceticism, austerity, renouncing the world, going into monasteries or hermits' caves and to top it all off, "death to oneself" or "the death of the ego." I personally was quite surprised to see an austere man like Swami Prajnanpad insist so strongly on the importance of daring to live, laying oneself open and rolling with the punches. It did not seem to go along with my understanding of Hindu spirituality. Yet there is a real risk here, one that I barely escaped on numerous occasions. It consists in trying to camouflage one's fear of living behind noble but untrue words. (Let me repeat that I too tried to do this. All I say is based on personal experience and on the truths which helped me become free. I consider myself neither competent nor qualified to speak of anything I have not personally experienced.) And so you fight against a feeling of suffocation in relation to your desire to lead a vast and full life, one rich in experience. We run the risk of deluding ourselves by turning our spiritual ideals into an excuse for our fear to live.

In Hindu terms, those who are *rajasic* (active) live intensely, but the goal is to become *sattvic* (calm, serene, internalized). I had therefore personally come to the conclusion that a sage in meditation – with closed eyes and a Buddha smile – was superior to a human being who dared to fully participate in life, who accepted all his inner drives and forces and gradually learned to master them. There undoubtedly lies a real risk here – that of deceiving oneself tremendously. I am not saying this to condemn or to accuse anyone; I too deceived myself. This is a risk I knew all too well, yet it is also a danger for you and for others – be they boys or girls, men or women. Please understand that I am speaking only in the name of wisdom, in relation to the highest form of spirituality: first be absolutely natural, then you can aspire to the supernatural. A well-known French saying puts it eloquently: *"Celui qui trahit la terre n'atteindra jamais le ciel"*: if you deny your earthly dimension, you will never attain your heavenly dimension.

It is a tragic mistake to go on suffocating the already considerably mutilated life force within ourselves, on the grounds that this is what a spiritual path demands. You tell yourself that by gradually withdrawing from the world, you will become the perfect example of a Sage who has renounced everything and bathes in the bliss of nirvana. This is a tremendous lie, based on denial and fear.

Those of you who are familiar with the writings of the famous (perhaps too famous) Rajneesh, know how much he insisted on daring to live. He used words like "celebrate" and "celebration," saying "make your life a celebration." Yet although I find certain pages in Rajneesh's books wonderful, I cannot quote as an authority a man whom I have never met nor an ashram in which I have never set foot. I abide by the masters who have acted as milestones along my own way.

All that you have heard from the mouth of the greatest sages or read in spiritual traditions is indeed true: a spiritual path definitely does include a fundamental aspect of death to oneself. One cannot remain a caterpillar and become a butterfly at the same time. Wings do not grow on a caterpillar's back – and they never will. But let us start at the beginning. If you are interested in real spirituality, and not in a caricature, you must first dare to fully recognize the enormous life force that exists in a child, and realize that this life force is divided against itself in you. It is true that a child's effervescence decreases as he grows older. No one expects an old man to be teeming with energy like a two-year-old; no one expects an old man to run all over and climb up on everything. But I am convinced that a large part of what is attributed to the natural aging process actually springs from the suffocation of our life force – first by teachers, then by life in general, and finally by ourselves. And I am convinced that no one can become a spiritual seeker or a yogi by suffocating his or her own life force.

If you have read a little about Hinduism, you know that the esoteric side of yoga is based on freeing a very powerful force, the *kundalini*, whose premature awakening in an insufficiently purified body can actually be dangerous. I am not a follower of hatha yoga or kundalini yoga, but I remember my confusion – being full of Ramdas, Ma Anandamayi and Ramana Maharshi – when in 1966 Swamiji tried to show me that my ideal of meditation and pure spirituality was nothing but a lie, as long as so many aspects of myself remained unfulfilled and frustrated.

That man, perhaps more than any other, was the embodiment of one who had renounced the world. As far as preconceived ideas we have about "sages" go, he was the opposite extreme to someone like Gurdjieff. I never did meet Gurdjieff, but the truth (or the legend) of the man inspired the first ten years of my spiritual quest. Gurdjieff had intensely experienced much adventure during his search for the truth at the end of the nineteenth century, when traveling itself was a real expedition. And he had the habit of destabilizing his disciples by plunging them into more-than-difficult situations, while at the same time telling them to dare to live fully. He has been accused of immorality, called a libertine and likened to Rasputin, but I remain convinced that a man capable of composing such pure and crystalline music cannot be limited to what his detracters said about him and that, on the contrary, he was a sage and a master in a disturbing and maybe even shocking way.

For the little Protestant that I used to be – on the one hand terribly anxious not to be criticized, trying to convince everyone how good and how nice I was, and on the other hand full to the brim of morals, boy scouting, fears and inhibitions – even though I did not meet Gurdjieff himself, all that I heard about his person, his teachings and the life force which emanated from him was nonetheless extremely beneficial. Still, it can be dangerous to claim that wisdom cannot be the fruit of frustration or of the fear of what one carries inside oneself. Such an attitude can lead to immorality and confusion – and that is just the opposite of the path to freedom.

Through the Gurdjieff teachings, I began to understand that there was no real discrepancy between wisdom – a word which had fascinated me ever since the age of 22 when I read Maeterlinck's *Wisdom and Destiny* – and existence in its most concrete forms. Some time later, I came into contact with a very different world. It was the world of Ma Anandamayi, of Ramdas, of Swamis in meditation on the banks of the Ganges or under a banyan tree . . . a world which for me was filled with beauty, harmony and detachment, one in which one's inner drives were immediately transformed into light and contemplation. Then I discovered that – apart from Ma Anandamayi, Ramdas or other sages worthy of admiration – many of those who stayed in ashrams and had become great meditators, be they Hindus or Europeans, had not actually attained any real freedom. They were certainly very impressive as they sat in silent and motionless meditation, and I did not doubt that something grand was going on inside them. But what really bothered me at the time was that aside from their daily hours of meditation, they were full of emotions, easily irritated, jealous or even completely off track. For example, on days when I was very tired and had asked them nothing, being too courteous to dare interrupt, I was forced to listen to them as they talked on and on, flinging speeches at me about *maya* (the unreality of the world) according to the teachings of Shankaracharya. Having no interest in psychology at the time, it did not occur to me that their verbal diarrhea could be a sign of repressed instincts and tendencies; nor did I see it as a kind of neurosis. Yet listening to them did make me feel ill-at-ease.

Later, I met Swami Prajnanpad in his poor and austere ashram. That man had successively renounced a political career (which many Indians would have liked to see him undertake as he was an intimate friend of Lal Bahadur Shastri, India's Prime Minister after Nehru), a university career, and finally a normal married life with a woman whom everyone agreed had been beautiful in her youth. Swamiji had shaken me to the roots – and a man with solid roots cannot be shaken – by convincing me that I myself was narrow, shallow and crippled. I was then forty years old. I thought at the time that I had been living a rather rich life, between my travels up and down the roads of India and my boldness in daring to challenge the sexual taboos of my youth. The words Swamiji pronounced were difficult to hear. Not only was I cut off from a depth which was of the metaphysical realm – the Essence beneath the appearance, the Real beneath the unreal, the One beneath the multiple, the Immutable beneath the changing (I was quite ready to hear that sort of language because it had been my staple diet) – but I was also cut off from my own vital depths, my own drives, my own instincts. For me, Swamiji represented the living Vedanta. No one could have suspected him of pleading his own cause; he had renounced the world and he remained motionless, still as a statue, for many hours each day. Yet that man battled with me in order to destroy the image I had made for myself of a sage, based on Ramdas and Ma Anandamayi. (Needless to say, to this day my veneration for those two sages is stronger than ever.) He forced me to admit that there was a dishonesty in my own spiritual life and that through meditation I was avoiding several aspects of real life and above all, several aspects of myself.

A practice called *lyings* played a specific role in Swamiji's teachings. This method, developed by Swamiji himself, consists in bringing to the surface certain childhood memories complete with their traumatic impact, in order to shed full light on how our fears first developed and how the idea became engraved in us that daring to trust our impulses can be dangerous or even reprehensible. Yet bringing the unconscious to light is not simply a question of alleviating our suffering by giving free rein to expressing the root cause of this suffering. It also entails understanding how the terrible law "It's wrong to live!" became engraved in us. A child's entire upbringing, even when it is not particularly religious, centers around "That's very good!" and "That's a bad thing to do, how could you!" A child quickly learns to divide the world in two, developing his own ideas about what is good (whatever pleases his parents and teachers) and what is bad (what displeases them). Thus begins the tragedy that Swamiji summed up in three words: crippled, narrow and shallow.

In your own eyes, what you did was good. In the eyes of Mom or Dad (whom you love and admire), what you did was bad. Since you have no doubt that Mom and Dad are right – and therefore that you are wrong – you can no longer believe in yourself. You become very wary of the life force inside you and of the forms it can take. And then we weave our prison, just as a spider weaves its web or a silkworm spins its cocoon. We are the ones who build our own prison. Starting with the impetus given by our teachers, we go on to progressively smother our impulses. Here, the words *"No denial, Arnaud"* became meaningful. God knows how much I wanted to deny all I saw inside myself that bothered me, all that seemed to contradict the wisdom which so fascinated me and which I saw so admirably reflected in all the Hindu sages and Tibetan rinpoches on whom I passionately focused my camera lens. I still remember one battle between Swamiji and myself where I felt that he wanted to lead me away from the spirituality which so enraptured me and to bring me back to a world which I claimed I wanted to surpass.

The fact is I had little chance of surpassing something with which I had never come face-to-face. This applies not only to the world of outward fascinations (women for men, men for women, success, money, power) but also to our own inner world. And if you live on a staple diet of René Guénon – as I did – with the idea of a luminous supra-consciousness and a dark and infernal infra-consciousness, then your resistance will be all the greater and misunderstandings will become almost inevitable.

Today, with all the strength of my conviction, I maintain that no one can reach the Kingdom of Heaven if he denies his natural energies. These energies are forces which propel us from child-hood. At puberty, they take the form of the sex drive, complete with its emotional aspect, and continue to manifest themselves through the fervor, the political activism, the dream of true love and all the noble causes which inflame an adolescent. We must rediscover within ourselves a life force which is not divided and struggling against itself. Swamiji often used the famous Sanskrit word *shakti* or *atmashakti* which signifies the basic energy of the Self, the unique and infinite energy revealed in all deaths and all births. Each death is the other face of a birth and each birth is the other face of a death. Our very metabolism is no more than a series of births and deaths on a physiological level. *Shakti*, energy, and "fullness of life." Swamiji also frequently used the word "richness." This does not mean a richness in relation to what you have, but rather in relation to what you are – a richness which cannot grow if you feel divided and in inner conflict. If one part of this life force is being used to repress or deny another, how much energy is left for self-expression?

The overall feeling that one is smothering – or even suffocating – is linked to this smothering of the life force itself. The life force has become divided between its attempts to externalize and a practically continuous repression which is thwarting these attempts. Our life force can indeed be refined and purified, but we should realize that it emanates from the highest reality. Manifestation (which is the expression of the Unmanifest) gives life to our cells, to our breathing, to our heartbeat and to the circulation of our blood; it underlies our entire physiology, and particularly our sexual energy. This energy, if it is no longer divided against itself, can be mastered, transformed, refined and used to serve a higher understanding. It can be used to serve what the situation demands, wisdom (*prajna*), or the will of God. But this can only happen if we become whole again, it can only happen if we dare to live.

Daring to live means no longer being afraid of oneself. It means turning around and going back down the path – untying the knots and lifting the barriers which condemned you to this fear of yourself and to the falsehood of a kind of disembodied spirituality made up of denial. It is a reunification which can become the starting point for self-possession and control. Then, once you have the courage to fully recognize what is within you, daring to live means developing the courage to leap into life; it means taking risks and receiving blows, knowing in advance that you will be exposed to the play of opposites: success/failure, happiness/unhappiness, praise/blame. You will surely have to face conditions which you previously considered painful, but you will be able to accept them because when you are "one with" a situation – whatever it may be – it can no longer affect you. And when suffering is accepted, it leads to a deep inner peace.

In actual fact, anyone with a great spiritual destiny will inevitably go through terrible moments of suffering, helplessness and hardship. Hindus often cite the proverb: "Man's extremity is God's opportunity." Perhaps you have had the experience of feeling that just as you were sinking to the very depths of heartbreak and despair, something in you let go and an unbelievable, unimaginable peace suddenly swept over you, even though the situation itself had not changed. In the brutal and magnificent words of Karlfried von Dürkheim: "What does not kill you, will make you grow." And it does indeed take a lot to kill someone. Not one of you here has died; not one of you has committed suicide. But, at one time or another, each of you has felt that he or she has suffered . . . and your suffering increased. You have felt that life was hard, that life was difficult, that life was painful.

Remember: when suffering is accepted, it is not painful; heartrending situations take on meaning and thrust us toward the Kingdom of Heaven within us. Once you have understood this, you will no longer be afraid to suffer. You must reach this stage. It must be very clear to you that if you follow the path because you are afraid to suffer, you will never progress. The goal on the path definitely is to suffer no more, to achieve a state of lasting peace and incomprehensible joy. Buddha said: "I teach only two things, O disciples: suffering (all the laws which help understand suffering) and the cessation of suffering." We all agree that the goal – bliss, *ananda*, freedom – is to suffer no more and to attain a state of universal, unchanging love. But the Path leads through suffering. The disciple is not one who tries to salvage all he hears at an ashram or a monastery so that he can put an end to his suffering;

he is one who is no longer afraid to suffer, one who does not fear to put himself into situations which may cause him suffering. At least he will have tried, he will have lived, he will have learned what life could or could not give him, he will have started to understand the truth of what is called *maya* (illusion), *moha* (attachment) and the play of attraction and repulsion. A disciple is one who agrees to suffer.

Someone who wants to explore the North Pole will agree to suffer from the cold; a mountaineer will agree to endure bad weather in high altitude and possibly be exposed to cold and fog; a navigator on the open sea will agree to brave a storm. One who is committed to the Path prefers to live and to suffer, rather than not to live so as not to suffer. I have not forgotten that inside me – hidden behind what remained of an overly strict upbringing and ideals which I do not deny – lay falsehood and the fear to suffer. I can see myself back in 1966, defending myself every inch of the way in front of Swamiji *("You are a coward, Arnaud")*, trying to convince myself that Swamiji was a psychoanalyst, not a guru. Yet at the same time, I was attracted by that man . . . with his goodness, his nobility, his cheerfulness. On the surface I was full of doubt. But deep down, I felt that I had to trust him.

The year 1966 was quite a painful one for me. Nonetheless, it was the year when my documentary film "The Message of the Tibetans" was nationally televised and when the producer named Arnaud Desjardins suddenly became quite famous in France. From the professional point of view, it was the year when the world changed for me. But it was also a year of combat with Swamiji: he forced me to live on a larger and wider scale, to recognize all that existed inside myself, to accept the deeper forces within me and to dare to throw myself more totally into the game of life . . . knowing all the while that I would be put to severe trials. This is the only way to really grow and one day to attain *all-embracing* realization, as they say in India, that which will completely shelter you from any backfire or disappointment, from any renewed outburst of despair or anger. If you want to feel totally invulnerable and totally unprotected at the same time, you must push through to your very limits. If certain *vasanas* (tendencies, impulses) have been held back or repressed and you have to constantly struggle against them, how can you be truly strong? How can you be in communion with life which is constantly bringing you face-to-face with yourself, if you cannot be in communion with your own reality? Swamiji forced me to see the ambition (and not the detachment) that I still held inside; he forced me to see my emotional and sentimental needs, my sexual needs . . . in short, all that is part of ordinary life. He forced me to bring everything out into broad daylight. Then he made me decide how I was going to live with it, while at the same time calling on me to exercise self-control and self-possession.

"Oh, Arnaud, can you miss the fullness of life?" Can you be satisfied with only half of life? Of course, if it is put that way, one's dignity – not even as a disciple but simply as a human being – answers "no." No, I will not live only half of life while I am embodied on this earth. And all that we like represents one half of life, while all that we are quite simply afraid of – because we associate it with suffering – represents the other half. The fullness of life is achieved through harmonizing, purifying and transcending life as a whole. But the difficulty I was constantly coming up against was that I sincerely considered my refusal of half of life to be the result of my own deliberate choice – whereas it was actually due to my timidity and weakness. (The mind is a tremendous liar but it is always sincere at the time.) I associated my refusal with my rationalized view of what was right or wrong. Yet this view itself was nothing other than the fruit of my childhood experiences, those of a child marked by the law described previously: "What I myself like is wrong; what my parents like is right." Can such a massive *samskara* (an impression engraved in us with a specific dynamic), branching out into so many separate *samskaras*, have any stable and truthful foundation?

But do not worry. I am not saying that the most cruel, beastly and vile impulses are there in everyone. And I am definitely not saying that becoming aware of these impulses will turn you into a torturer, a rapist or a swindler. Such fears are once again the lies of the mind and they are totally beside the point; the point is to no longer be afraid of the life inside you.

⁓ · ⁓

It is a sacrilege to be afraid of the life force within you – your vital energy – even if this life force caused you difficulty when you were a child or an adolescent. It is blasphemy; it is refusing God himself. Whether or not we want it to be so, this world – just as it is – is the expression and manifestation of God. Certain words in Genesis are intolerable unless they are deeply reflected upon: "And God saw that his Creation was good." What? God saw that his Creation was good? But just take a look at his Creation! Big animals eat little ones, drought devastates harvests and an earthquake can cause the ruin of an entire population; human beings are incapable of loving each other and parents, who mean only to educate their children, end up mutilating them. . . not to mention all the suffering endured in times of war or revolution and all the oppression such times include.

"And God saw that his Creation was good." In fact, if we accept creation as a whole, we will see that it has meaning, over and above what shocks or scandalizes us and beyond contradictions and opposites. The first way to apply the truth "God saw that his Creation was good," is to accept yourself completely, in the whole of your being, as a creature, that is, as a creation or an expression of God (or of energies of God as the Orthodox Church specifies). Yin and yang, night and day, sun and rain, heat and cold . . . everything is within us. And only by accepting ourselves as a whole can we attain the *shakti*: light, love, invulnerability, peace, the infinite. These are just words that attempt to describe a reality you may feel attracted to, a reality which is promised to you.

You can only reach the Unmanifest through the Manifestation. You can only attain *atman* or *brahman* through *shakti* (energy) and through the fullness of this energy. If you look closely, this energy first seems contradictory: building and destroying, birth and death – things which are commonly called dualities. At times this energy takes the form of what you have been taught to recognize as good in yourself, at times it takes that of what you have been taught to consider bad: certain desires, certain thoughts, certain fantasies, certain impulses. It expresses itself through thoughts which obsess and torture you, and also through very happy and optimistic states of mind. It is when you feel so good that your heart swells in your chest . . . and it is anguish. In short, it takes opposite forms.

Yet what is essential – what will allow you to go from an ordinary level to a higher level – is that this energy can be discovered *at its source* as the life force which is beyond *or rather before* the play of opposites. The purely positive power of this energy is something you can feel inside, it is something you can develop an inner awareness of. It is an absolute positive for which there is no negative, as Swamiji one day said to me. At its source, this energy in us – *atmashakti* – is merely a force of expression, before this expression becomes linked to Brahma (the creative aspect of all that is universally manifested) or to Shiva (the destructive aspect).

All you have ordinarily experienced, both within yourself and outside yourself, has been "pairs of opposites": good/bad, agreeable/disagreeable, pleasant/unpleasant, right/wrong, success/failure. But as long as you remain a prisoner of the world of dualities, you will be enslaved to a longing for the happy aspect of duality and a fear of its painful aspect. It is a dead end. You must rise to another plane. And in order to find the Ultimate, to find rest in the light, the calm of a lake without ripples, the ocean which expresses itself in each wave, you must discover within yourself that energy which has not yet become divided into opposite polarities and which has not yet become specialized: the life force itself.

Let me emphasize something: life is entirely positive. It is the manner in which life is expressed that takes on the form of creation or destruction. And we remain prisoners of that level. Life is immortal, Life is eternal, Life is infinite. Because you know no more than its surface, you see your own personal life as being inevitably condemned to opposites. But if you stop being afraid of yourself, if you do not limit yourself to a few ideas about generosity and self-control (which are right when they are correctly understood, but which can become a basis for our hypocrisy in relation to ourselves), if you are true to yourself as you are today, then in yourself you can discover non-dual life, the disappearance of opposites. (The Bhagavad Gita insists strongly on these opposites, which are called *dvandvas* in Sanskrit.)

This non-duality, this harmonious reconciliation of opposites seen in the diagram of yin and yang clasped together in a circle, this transcending of opposites, happens not only on the Absolute or Unmanifest level, on the level of Emptiness (*shunyata*). It is also expressed through the vital force, through energy. This can save you. This is the first discovery you can make; this is the first level on which you can base yourself.

You cannot become established in the great silence of nirvana unless you first become rooted in fundamental energy, before it divides into opposite polarities. Do not seek only the supra-conscious state found in meditation, a state in which you feel detached from everything – even if this is a real state which will one day underlie your entire existence, no matter what trials life may bring. Although you have every right to long for it, you will never attain this state if you refuse the way in which it is expressed. And it is through the *shakti*, the almost terrifying life force which sustains you, that this supra-conscious state expresses itself.

It is true that this first stage can be reached through certain forms of meditation, namely the whole approach popularized in the West by Karlfried von Dürckheim. I personally saw Dürckheim's approach confirmed by both Japanese masters and Tibetan yogis. This approach consists in rediscovering the life force within the pelvis, within the abdomen, in the hara – through breathing, particularly while exhaling.

A very precious form of meditation consists in not directly seeking the *atman* (the absolute) but rather in first searching for the life force inside oneself in a non-conflictual and undivided state. And it is easier to discover this life force than to attain the *atman*, which is its source. This is the key itself to yoga: taking the road of what is manifested back in the opposite direction; going from the more gross to the more subtle, from the multiple back to one. The "Manifestation" is an expression of energy, so it is possible to travel back down the path of energy in us. In meditation, you first get the impression of a kind of force, a power, a non-conflictual vitality which precedes any division into positive/negative or creation/destruction. What you feel is something that comes before opposites.

The highest state of consciousness available to us is to become established on this level of non-duality and non-contradiction. It can also be called the Unchangeable or the Indestructible. In this state, the very question of death itself no longer arises. Like others before me, I have tried to describe this state by comparing it to a screen onto which a film is projected or to Shiva in meditation as opposed to Shiva dancing. But to become permanently established on this level, so that it will underlie all the events of your life and allow you to "dis-identify" totally with the character you play (one who has a given name, past, predisposition and karma), you must turn and travel back down the path of what is manifested in order to return to the unmanifest. First you leave behind the usual level of oppositions and contradictions in the field of emotions, sensations, ideas and moods. Then you rediscover your own fundamental energy. And finally, aided by this *shakti*, you return to the *atman* (which is itself the source the *shakti*). But for a start, accept yourself as a whole, without fear. Meditation is thus not only the search for the Unmanifest, it is also the search for the origin of all that is manifested. It is the search for energy itself.

It is true that you cannot devote your life to simply being aware of the great life force within you, a force which becomes progressively more intense and is totally reassuring, the same life force that nurtured you as an embryo and afterwards as a baby. You must also live your own karma or destiny (in any case *prarabdhakarma* – that karma which will inevitably bear fruit, whether or not one attains enlightenment or inner awakening).

But on the path of wisdom, one thing is certain: you must dare to live. It is no use hoping for that supreme "de-suffocation," hoping for the infinite and for all the grand spiritual realities you have heard of, unless you dare to play the game of life, unless you dare to open up and take risks. Look at the risks some take in the mountains, on the sea or in car racing. Look at the risks that you are driven to take by the madness of your mind, or by a passionate love affair that jeopardizes the balance of your entire existence as well as the happiness of those around you and perhaps also your financial situation. Look at the risks you take mechanically, when you are simply carried away by a series of actions and reactions for which you are unable to take the consequences; you moan and cry for help although you were the one who attracted your fate, you were the one who got yourself into the situation. And because you are afraid, you hope that spirituality will provide you with some good reasons to run from life. All those risks which you so often take unconsciously – take them consciously.

I will dare. Will I be criticized? Yes, I will be criticized. Perhaps I will suffer and things will not go as I had planned. Everything is dangerous. It is not possible to live fully, unless there is some danger. You cannot experience wisdom if you refuse experience. Being in love is dangerous. "Ah, but the sage. . . " Granted, one does not imagine a sage being in love in the ordinary sense of the word. But at the age of twenty, one cannot pretend to be a sage. Nor even at the age of forty. And Swamiji certainly made that clear for me, strongly and intensely, at a certain stage of my progression.

You cannot live without taking the risk of suffering – until the time comes when you discover the secret which places you beyond suffering, whatever the circumstances of your life may be. It is this secret which I try to share with you and which underlies every page of every book published in my name. No matter what happens, you are going to suffer. So why not accept it deliberately once and for all? "I will suffer, I will welcome suffering as an enriching experience, as the fullness of life. I will see it as a way back to my own truth, I will turn it into a path of purification, I will use it to help me transcend suffering." I will suffer with the feeling: "may the will of God be done" or "today it is God's will that I suffer because it suits who I am just now and this is where my hope lies one day to reach what is beyond all else." From there on, you can live without fear: *"The way is not for the coward, Arnaud."* My own cowardice was the fear to live that I carried inside, a poverty rooted in my childhood and upbringing, which Swamiji showed me in broad daylight and which I justified through lies. . . using spiritual truths which were right, but truths which my mind had latched onto to help it cheat.

Once this truth had been assimilated, Swamiji brought in another notion – that of dignity. As soon as I become whole again, as soon as I choose integral truth, as soon as I am ready to live and to take the blows in order to achieve freedom, I find myself confronted with the demand for dignity. What is in keeping with my dignity and what is below my dignity?

And if you are brave enough to stop repressing things and to stop deceiving yourself, if in meditation you are willing to seek the life force instead of searching solely for the silence of nirvana, then the word dignity will quickly take on meaning. That precious word puts your entire moral code onto another level: "It is below my dignity." But this springs from an inner conviction. It is no longer the voice of your parents that you hear inside you, nor that of theology, nor that of imposed moral standards. It is a voice which arises from within, one which is pure and right and whose function is to guide you. It is below my dignity to act in such a way today. However, what will be below your dignity in a few years time, may not be so today. *"Be faithful to yourself, as you are situated here and now"* – with the hope that, in a few years time, you will no longer be the same man or the same woman as you are today. And although today it may be impossible for you to attain detachment and a different state of being (even though you want to), it will become possible for you tomorrow.

However you cannot accede to this new freedom as long as one element of denial remains in you, as long as you are in fear of that wonderful life force sustaining you.

Swamiji gave me the word *dignity* as if it were a treasure. He spoke of *"you yourself in your own intrinsic dignity."* And I am sharing that word with you so that you will be firmly convinced that I am not asking you to unleash uncontrollable forces and irresistible impulses, so that you will not feel I am asking you to transgress morals and taboos. That would make you take fright immediately. Swami Prajnanpad made these words permanently resound in me, "Is this in keeping with my dignity?" They are words which no longer come from an outside voice but from a conviction arising from deep within. You will see how much the word "dignity" will support you, if you stop lying to yourself and rediscover the fullness of your life force. "This is where I am today; I will cheat no more." And then I act. I accept myself as I am and no longer pretend to be a false Ramana Maharshi or a caricature of Ma Anandamayi. (This is always a danger when one is truly attracted to spirituality but not yet completely established in truth.) I stop being afraid of myself; I detach myself from my fear of myself. I dare to want. I dare to feel my own strength; I dare to feel my impulses rise up inside. Dignity: what will I do? how will I act? what is right for me today? what will help me progress?

You must reconcile everything: the manifested and the unmanifest, the static and the dynamic, the male and the female, the active and the passive. Obviously these are only words, a string of words, whereas truth must be felt inside oneself, both as an experience and as a reality.

The message I insist on today is this: stop being emotionally crippled and shallow; stop living in untruth. And, at the same time, I immediately add the word "dignity." Without it, you will go astray; you will think you are free because you are turning up your nose at your childhood morals and treading your neighbor underfoot. Once you discover energy or the life force inside yourself in its yet uncontradictory state, the world of opposites takes on new meaning. Immediately you begin to see deeper than the play of opposites. Immediately you begin to catch a glimpse of the essence behind the appearance, the depth beneath the surface. You start to see, as Genesis says, that this creation – which seems so cruel – is good.

～·～

Creation, just as it is, will lead us to the ultimate. When you become capable of discovering within yourself a state of being without conflict, you will know that ultimate reality underlies polarities because you will have experienced it by not denying the life inside you. Behind all the heartrending contradictions of this world, behind all the suffering, a meaning you had missed until now will reveal itself: an absolute positiveness, eternity, immortality, a totally luminous reality. But you cannot try to discover it without following the way of truth. This implies starting from the grosser forms of energy, going toward the more and more subtle forms, and ultimately toward the source of energy itself – the indescribable silence of the depths. Ah, how much those who think they are afraid of death, are actually afraid of life! They are afraid of themselves. How little you believe in yourselves! What wariness of yourself, when it is not downright self-hatred, life has instilled in you! What a mistake! Dare to live. Begin by simply daring to breathe. Dare to open up. Dare to feel. The more you fear the richness, the fullness and the force of life, the more of a slave you become to your head and your thoughts. The mind is essentially the fruit of this fear to live. You take refuge in a world of ideas, because it is a subjective one in which you can do what you want. Thoughts correspond to our repetitive tendencies which we can keep turning over indefinitely. The more you live, the less you think; the more you think, the less you live. Those who are harassed by the whims of the mind, cut off from reality, can reflect on this: it is not thinking that is important, it is feeling.

Why does the word "feeling" sound suspicious to those who pride themselves on their knowledge of spirituality or who are genuinely attracted by the highest forms of spirituality? To be afraid to feel is actually to consider that Creation is evil and that one must definitely not play the game of nature. But you can only discover the ultimate secret by participating in the cosmic game, which is underlied and animated by God himself.

So the more you think, the less you feel and the more you feel, the less you think. One of the first things that can help you to live is to start daring to feel – without fear – even just on a sensual, sensorial level; little by little, the all-powerful intellect has cut us off from sensuality and sensoriality. And it is particularly necessary to accept the two poles of reality in ourselves so as to harmonize them: male and female, yin and yang, action and contemplation.

The less you dare to live and the less you dare to feel, the more you take refuge in the male aspect of existence (whether you are male or female) and the more you try to act . . . to do something . . . to be always doing something. This is just the opposite of meditation and the opposite of contemplation – it is the neurosis of activism. "What is there to do?" To the extent that, even on the Way, the master must strive to find constantly new exercises for you to do! The more you privilege your male aspect over your female aspect, the more you cut yourself off from feeling and condemn yourself to thinking. But male values of action are somehow reassuring, be it neurotically.

On the other hand, female values (centered on openness) have quite a frightening dimension. What will I open up to? Receptivity and welcoming seem dangerous! And opening up to what is expressing itself inside you is also very dangerous. It is no problem to read *Toward the Fullness of Life* by Arnaud Desjardins with the chapters on one's male and female sides, or to read what Dürckheim says about "arrow consciousness" and "cup consciousness." In a disastrous way, the modern world has privileged male values over female ones, reason over sensitivity, the head in all domains, and action over contemplation. Feminism does not mark a return of respect for female values. Instead, it gives women a chance to be even more male than men themselves, with the consequence that everyone rejects female values, even though they are precious for both men and women.

To live is to make room for these female values as quickly as possible and as completely as possible, and to ask yourself what meaning the word "openness" has for you. The heart cannot expand unless it opens. There is a saying that "Islam is the expanding of the chest," but even the chest cannot expand unless it opens. To open up means to open up without cheating. You cannot close all the doors – both inside and out – and then open yourself up to the grace of God. The grace of God itself can come to you through the most cruel trials . . . through betrayal by those you trust, through rejection, through all that you would previously have considered terrible. All is Grace. Always open up, it is always God who is knocking. Opening up means opening up with all one's heart. Developing the female values of welcome and receptiveness means developing them in every way. This consists in no longer protecting oneself. If someone slaps me on one check, I will turn the other, as Christ said. And it means opening up to your inner life force, instead of performing all kinds of acrobatics to do meditations that will help you escape the fears you carry inside.

Part of your practice can include certain kinds of psychotherapy. *Lyings* provide an opening to the life force in its conflictual aspect. In *lyings*, you can sob over the greatest joys you ever felt because they did not last; you can dare, today, to confront and re-experience deep sufferings – ones which may have nailed you to the spot and totally demolished you – so as to be free of them. And meditation is an opening to the non-dual, non-conflictual vital impulse. It is simply discovering: I am living! I am alive, animated by an infinite energy which is not my life, but Life. That is what counts. You go beyond your life – in which you are inevitably smothering no matter how successful you may be – to discover that you are an expression or form of universal Life, divine energy, the same which animates the birds that sing, the leaves that quiver in the wind, the little green buds that come out in spring and the life in each atom. In us, this energy takes on its most evolved form, *prajna* (consciousness, wisdom and understanding).

Swami Prajnanpad's *lying* is an opening to the life force in its conflictual form so that you will no longer be afraid of this contradictory form. Having dared to confront suffering face-to-face in *lyings*, you can then confront it in life without fear or denial. And little by little, you will free yourself from suffering.

Meditating does not just mean seeking the emptiness and silence of the Unmanifest. It is seeking non-duality and non-conflict in the very feeling that you exist. From then on, you become a complete human being and you can grow, blossom and unfold. You can feel the fullness of the life force arise in you. Uproot that old unconscious fear of yourself, that old childish fear, "What stupid things I am capable of, unless I repress them! The more narrowly I live, the less I risk being punished." And should either the teachings or the guru take over from these inhibitions – with "the death of the ego," "mortification," "renouncement" and "sacrifice" – then spirituality turns into nothing but delusion and you end up nowhere.

You cannot love another unless you love yourself. You cannot love yourself if you are afraid of yourself. You cannot avoid fearing yourself if you are running away from yourself. And if you are running away from yourself, you are wearing yourself out trying to stay on the surface of yourself and on the surface of life. How can you possibly reach a deeper level?

Do not be afraid. The life force within us, within you, within everyone is purely reassuring if it is discovered at its source. If you rediscover life, if you dare to live, if you dare to open up, you will see how everything that dominates your life today – fears, sufferings, tragedies, attachments, emotions, disturbing thoughts – forms a prison that will start to release its bonds.

Choose to live.

2

AN INNER STRUCTURE

To live fully, you must *be*. Of course, by simply using the personal pronouns "I" or "me," we show that we are. Yet no matter how revolting or incongruous it may seem to one's "ego," esoteric doctrines affirm that man *is not*. He "is not" in the sense that he is not a unified subject, master of his reactions and capable of acting consciously. Knowing through experience that you cannot count on yourself, you are afraid of life because you are afraid of yourself (more or less, that is, because in the relative everything is always more or less). It is up to you to give birth to this unified and stable being and to get it to assert itself. Then – freely, deliberately and lucidly – you will be able to do, to receive and to give. You will be able to give yourself.

In order to give oneself, one must belong to oneself.

What you receive from me, the help that you can expect from me, results from a training which draws from different sources. I began with the Gurdjieff groups, with whom I remained from 1950 until 1964. Each time I have a chance to reread a passage from *In Search of the Miraculous*, I find the book even more remarkable than I had guessed in my youth, and I see a number of parallels that can be drawn between the teachings of Swami Prajnanpad and those of Gurdjieff. I met too with various masters of extremely diverse traditions. Among these were Tibetan rinpoches, whom I encountered between 1964 and 1967, when it was still possible to come into rather close contact with them. I met Karmapa, Khentse Rinpoche, Kangyur Rinpoche, Lopon Sonam Zangpo and many others whom I was able to question – through the services of a first-class interpreter – at a time when there was little contact between Tibetans and Westerners. It is clear to me now that my present convictions are a synthesis of all the different sources with which I have come into contact. Last of all, my exchanges with disciples and apprentice-disciples have allowed me to verify how valid these teachings really are, both as to the power of the "mind" and the possibility of escaping from the mind itself.

The training I received, or the potential to transmit, has three aspects which I see as a whole although for you they may appear different. The first aspect is psychological. There is no doubt that Swamiji was what we would call a psychologist. The study of *manas* (the mind) and *chitta* (the *psychism*: conscious and unconscious memories) can be likened to psychology.

The second aspect is quite simple, although it is capital. You could call it the religious or mystical aspect. It consists in unburdening the heart of the coarse emotions which encumber it. At a time when I was fascinated by esoteric studies, I had to bow down to a lay brother of Bellefontaine Abbey who barely had a high school diploma yet radiated peace and serenity and had a light in his eyes that many of those who swore by the Vedanta and the "yoga of knowledge" lacked.

Then there is a third aspect, an esoteric one. This on the contrary includes certain unusual conceptions normally passed down from master to disciple, and often in a certain secrecy. Each of these three aspects has played an important role in my life. What I would like to tell you today falls more specifically under what could be considered the esoteric aspect of the way, and comes close to the Gurdjieff teachings. Year after year I have had the chance to test and verify a number of conclusions found in the book *In Search of the Miraculous*. I would like to share these conclusions with you. Being the fruit of my own synthesis, they are my personal convictions and so, in a sense, they are neither the teachings of Gurdjieff nor those of Swamiji.

Some years ago, having already practiced a good deal of yoga, I sought out yogis in conformity with the great tradition who had consecrated their lives to spirituality and wisdom and who based their development on Patanjali's *Yoga-Sutras* or the *Hatha yoga pradipika.* One day in 1963, it was given to me to meet one such yogi. Considering I had already spent twelve years in the Gurdjieff groups plus nearly a year of my life with Ma Anandamayi, I was all the more shaken by the advice he gave me: *"What you need is to build an inner structure."* When you have been doing spiritual practices for twelve years, such a statement is a little difficult to take!

I never saw that yogi again but what he had said stayed with me for a long time. I felt an imperative need to find the connection between two approaches which seemed contradictory to me at the time. On the one hand, there was Gurdjieff's approach, or that of the yogi, which implied "building an inner structure" and making various efforts situated in time, so as to create something which does not exist today; on the other hand, there was the classic Vedantic approach which insisted untiringly and almost exclusively on a totally different idea – that we are *already* wisdom and that we need only to awaken. In Ramana Maharshi's words, "You are already free; your only mistake is that you believe you are not free."

One year later, in 1964, when I first came into contact with Tibetan masters in Darjeeling, Kalou Rinpoche told me: *"You are peace, you are truth."* And five months after that, Swamiji repeated to me word for word, *"You are truth"* as he struck me on the chest. I had just told him: "I realize that peace is deep within me, that truth is deep within me . . ." And he had immediately rectified: *"No, you are peace, you are truth, you are wisdom."* According to the Vedanta, what we are looking for is already there, just as we are already naked beneath our clothes and need only to take them off to discover that nakedness. Whatever has a beginning in time inevitably has an end, whatever has been created can be destroyed by an opposing cause, whatever has been composed will be decomposed; nothing other than ultimate Reality, the absolutely simple, pure Consciousness, Brahman, deserves your efforts. There is no point in concerning oneself with what has a beginning in time because this keeps us within causation (a cause produces an effect) and on the plane of effort – even if this is one of the more subtle planes of the manifestation. What Swamiji proposed was *"to be free from all matter, both gross and fine."*

How can one reconcile this Vedantic approach (seeking what Buddha called "that which is unborn, uncreated, devoid of aggregates and non-becoming") with the need to create an inner structure? I must admit that for years there seemed to me to be an incompatibility between the two approaches that I could not resolve because I was unable to drop either side of the contradiction. I certainly did feel that I had a real need to build an inner structure. This is what I want to talk about today. I am sure you feel how important it is.

~··~

Before delving into this subject, there are a couple of esoteric concepts which must be acknowledged. The first is that there is no real difference between matter and energy. Modern scientists affirm this point but I personally am not a scientist. Matter which Hindus qualify as fine or subtle can be felt to be equally matter and energy. (This of course does not concern ordinary matter which can be perceived with the five senses.) As an illustration, the radio and television waves passing through the room at this very moment have a certain materiality because they can be measured, but it is a materiality which is "subtle" or "fine." *Prana*, that energy which is accumulated by breathing consciously, can just as well be experienced as matter or as energy. In India it is taught that *sarvam annam* (everything is food), but at the same time there is a distinction between two types of food: food for the coarse or gross body – which is a subject for anatomy and physiology – and food for the subtle body.

This idea of a subtle body deserves a little attention. Why do we use the same word "body" (*sharir*) to indicate the gross body (which will decompose and be eaten by worms or burned on a funeral pyre), as well as the subtle body and the causal body? To describe three different realities, India uses the same word, *sharir*, which is always translated into English as "body". What I am saying here is not just Hindu learning, it is something I consider quite necessary for you on your spiritual path, however you may conceive of your "liberation" at present.

Under ordinary conditions, experience shows us that we do not have control over how we function. It is this irrefutable fact that tradition calls blindness, illusion or ignorance. We live in sleep and implacable laws rule over us. Psychology studies these laws and we daily bear the brunt of them when we are sad or depressed or when we lose the serenity we tasted a moment before without knowing why we are suddenly anxious. Even though man is overwhelmingly mechanical, he does not recognize this and imagines that he is free. Take a look at what you observe in yourself or in others: not only do events have power over you, but your mind, which carries you away in any which direction, reigns over your life. Suddenly – although you do not always know why – there is a gap between you and reality; you no longer see truth as it is, you are ill-at-ease and aggressive, even though you did not deliberately choose to be, of course. Instead of seeing the mind for what it is, or an emotion for what it is, you identify with these inner phenomena and they manipulate you without your knowledge. Gurdjieff called a human being who is subject to this bondage a "man-machine"; Swamiji taught that man is a puppet, with life pulling the strings by the changes of mood which it imposes on him. Existence gives you orders through what reacts in you in the form of various emotions and compulsive thoughts.

This is where the following words come in: *"You do not live in the world, you live in your world"*; you do not see the situation as it is, you see the situation which your mind projects. No one sees Jacqueline; each one sees *his* or *her* Jacqueline. Life presses the buttons and pulls the levers of the machines we are. Who, of his own will, can stop being anxious if he is anxious, being humiliated if he is humiliated or being wounded if he is wounded? You must study the precise workings of this mechanism which forces you to obey outside stimuli. At one time or another, you will each be fully aware: "I am not my own master; moods that I cannot control make a slave of me." If you could choose, you would definitely choose an open heart, serenity and confidence; you would choose the happiest and most divine feelings – not those negative emotions which sweep over you.

What power do you have at the beginning of the "Way"? None. *"It is the status of a slave,"* said Swamiji. Modern psychology studies the mechanicalness of the different ways humans function on the physical, physiological and mental levels (levels corresponding to the Hindu description of the *Koshas*) and uses the term "psychosomatic" to describe the close interdependence existing between the psychism and the body. Swamiji called this the *"body-mind complex."* The interdependence of the psychism and the body – through the nervous system, the brain and the endocrine glands – dictates a whole set of reactions: be happy, be unhappy, throw yourself in that unwise direction, burn what you adored, destroy with one hand what you have built with the other, act against your own interests . . . . Unbreakable chains of cause and effect are at work.

Under these conditions, as Gurdjieff said, we do not have the right to say "I." Not "I" want or "I" decide, but rather, within me, "it" wants, "it" decides and then "it" wants the opposite and "it" does not keep the decision it took. Experience will prove this to you if you observe yourself and others around you. Gurdjieff called this "the horror of the situation." Swamiji said *"Life, what a tragedy!"* or *"Mind, what a tragedy!"*

This complex organization that forms our make-up – the physical, emotional and mental – is not autonomous. Man as studied in physiology, endocrinology, neurology, psychology and sociology is forced to obey orders that are foreign to his lucid awareness.

And building an inner structure means building a subtle reality in ourselves; it means building a body, in the Hindu sense of the word, which no longer obeys these orders. Building a structure involves little by little setting up an inner organism independent of outside events and of the disturbances they cause in us. One day in 1966 Swamiji told me: *"You are an amorphous crowd."* The word "amorphous" has a specific meaning in chemistry: it is the opposite of "crystallized." *"You are a multitude, a multiplicity lacking form and lacking structure."* Thus, although Swamiji always insisted on the Vedantic affirmation *"You are already peace, wisdom, serenity and love,"* he also insisted on the necessity of no longer being an amorphous crowd but rather an organic, coherent and stable whole. Until this structure is forged, you will obey the orders of your destiny no matter what efforts you make. Your efforts will indeed help create this missing structure, but do not delude yourself: the ordinary psychosomatic, body-mind complex as a whole is a slave. The process or method which leads to freedom is the same for everyone, be it a Zen or Trappist monk, an ascetic or a yogi. To function on a different level – free from emotions and mood changes, no longer identified or carried away – it is always necessary to progressively create an autonomous "body."

~ · · ﹀

Let us synthesize all that has been said up until now. From the start, the possibility of awareness, fullness and love that we are seeking already exists in us. But we are rarely in contact with this deep Reality and even if we momentarily attain a much finer level of being – one characterized above all by a total absence of fear – we do not remain on this level; such is the painful experience of all who frequent sages. They have the impression that they are living in a state of grace when they go off and stay at an ashram but once back home, six months later, they find themselves worried and anxious – maybe even playing with thoughts of suicide – wondering how they could have felt they had risen so high, to end up falling so low.

If you read *In Search of the Miraculous* , and I recommend that
you do, you will see that Gurdjieff speaks of various centers in man:
on the one hand, the emotional, intellectual, instinctive/moving
and sex centers which everyone has experienced, and on the other,
two centers of a different order: the "higher emotional center" and
the "higher intellectual center." These two latter centers are situated well beyond what we call emotions and intellect. They are
already fully formed and function perfectly, but man enters into
contact with them only very rarely. If he does, he cannot maintain
this contact because he is riveted to the level of the ordinary centers
which work in a much grosser manner. The theory of ordinary and
higher centers is very interesting because it explains why human
beings, who know only the ordinary centers, cannot communicate
with Reality even though it already exists within them. If one gear-
wheel in a car turns very quickly while another turns very slowly,
it will be impossible to engage the gears. In the same way, the higher
emotional and intellectual centers radiate at a level of subtlety with
which ordinary emotions and thoughts cannot connect. Much work
is needed to purify and refine the grosser functions to enable us
to maintain contact with the higher centers.

What Gurdjieff called the higher emotional center, Swamiji –
giving the word a very noble meaning – called love. But in contrast
with the ordinary emotional center (which sometimes likes, sometimes dislikes; is sometimes cheerful, at others sad; sometimes
accepts and at others refuses), the higher emotional center does
not have a negative half. It is normal for the ordinary intellectual
center sometimes to say yes, sometimes to say no; it is normal for
the instinctive center sometimes to say yes, sometimes to say no. If
you eat something poisonous, your stomach will automatically vomit
it out; if you put your hand on a scorching hotplate, the moving
center says no and, without even thinking, you take your hand off;
if you are offered unsuitable equipment, your intelligence will
examine it and then refuse it. Conversely, the higher emotional
center and the higher intellectual center, says Gurdjieff, have no

negative half – only YES, a pure and total vision of reality (isness, suchness, thatness). It is easy to see the parallel with Swamiji's teaching. "Being ONE with" is the Way which leads to the higher emotional center. The intellectual center, even in a sage, sometimes says yes, sometimes says no; his moving center sometimes says yes, sometimes no. Why should a sage let his hand grill on a red-hot metal plate? But the heart is always one with what is. It is always YES, always love, always non-duality.

Here we come back to the need for an inner structure. An adequate instrument must be put at the disposition of the already-perfect higher emotional center or the reality which we already are. It must be an instrument with a level of quality independent of conditions and circumstances, free of the implacable play of physiological, mental and emotional reactions. And this instrument is in fact the subtle body which can be structured little by little, until one day it crystallizes. The Sanskrit word for the subtle body is *sukshma sharir*. It corresponds to certain koshas called *manomayakosha* and *vijnanamayakosha* which make up one's entire psychological way of functioning. An ordinary man or woman's subtle body is composed of nothing but reaction. Instead of describing this as amorphous or shapeless, Hindus sometimes call it a "bundle."

Just as it is possible to develop muscles and to limber up one's physical body through exercise, so too is it possible to form this inner structure through a *sadhana*. A sadhana always involves a series of conscious efforts. Your subtle body can thus be structured little by little until an autonomous inner body is created, one which functions independently and no longer obeys outside orders. Consequently, it will become not only possible but easy to achieve a state of equanimity, even temper, or inner stability which seemed out of reach for so long. But until this subtle body crystallizes and takes its autonomous and non-dependent form, immense effort and very great awareness must be exercised, so that you will no longer be ruled by your mechanisms. The passage from an amorphous crowd to a crystallized inner structure can only result from your spiritual practice.

It is here that the concept of fine matter comes in. Fine matter is subtle matter which can be considered both energy and matter. This fine matter can completely permeate all the cells of the physical body whereas the subtle materiality of television waves goes through our bodies without being assimilated.

We simultaneously receive, treat, and respond to, information. Receiving is a female value; intervening in the world is a male value. For each of these functions, energy is necessary. We readily admit that energy is needed to plow the earth or to shout if we are angry. But energy is also needed to feel. If you lack energy, you can no longer receive impressions. Remember that point because it is very important. We do not hesitate to admit that energy is needed to sing, to reflect, to get angry – even to brood over things or to despair – yet we often forget that perceiving, receiving and appreciating also require energy.

Each center requires specific energy in order to function – be it the intellectual center, the emotional center, the moving center or the sex center – and if one form of energy is lacking, we are no longer able to perceive certain sensations. For example, a landscape which you have always found beautiful may leave you completely indifferent and no longer affect you, but if you see the same landscape one week later, you may once again be struck by how beautiful it is. Or you might put on a record which you are fond of and feel nothing, simply because you lack the particular energy corresponding to that perception. A week later, you may again appreciate the same piece. This too applies to sexual energy. If a man momentarily lacks sexual energy, the most beautiful woman in the world can dance naked in front of him and it will leave him just as indifferent as if someone were showing him the cross section of a car engine. But three days later, once the energy has returned, if a pretty woman dances naked in front of him, he will receive a very strong impression which generally activates the process of desire, with emotions eventually grafting themselves onto it. A certain amount of energy is required to receive foods of impressions, whatever these may be.

⌣ · ⌣

"*Sarvam annam,*" "Everything is food." These are some of the most important words in the Upanishads. The various Hindu paths do not all interpret this saying in the same way. For a follower of Tantra (and I beg you not to mistake Tantra for nothing but the mystic eroticism which has a certain popularity), everything is food: if someone insults you, that is food. . . as long as you know how to digest and assimilate it. This is what Hindus and Tibetans call digesting poisons. Normally, being insulted does not constitute very nice food. It is easier to transform the sight of Ma Anandamayi into wisdom than to transform insults into wisdom. But everything is food. If you knew how to do it, you could find nourishment in everything, even in the insults of someone who vomits his hate and aggressiveness onto you.

In every spiritual path, it is absolutely necessary that a part of these foods which we use to perceive and respond to perceptions be preserved so that it will be deposited in us, little by little, until there is saturation and finally crystallization. Therefore part of the energy (which is both energy and matter) furnished by the different foods, must not be consumed; it must instead be saved so it can be refined, just as crude oil is refined to produce premium gasoline. We thus develop an autonomous inner structure and life can no longer give us orders (suffer, get angry, be afraid, hate. . .), whereas the ordinary body-mind complex will always obey these commands. This crystallization process is not proper to the Orient. A Trappist monk also gains experience of it even if he does not describe it in the same way.

For crystallization to take place, the substance we draw from the three foods – the *prana* contained in inhaled air, food and the impressions which come to us – should not be used solely to function. And remember that there are two aspects to functioning: being sensitive, perceiving and appreciating (on an instinctive, motor, emotional, intellectual or sexual level) and subsequently being able to respond. If someone lacks energy, even insults will have no affect on him. This is neither freedom nor wisdom; it is just a deficiency that hampers one's capacity to perceive.

What can we do so that the energy provided by the different foods will no longer be consumed by existence in the form of excitement, sorrow and anger through the different interests which come along, such as our professional or love life? And how can we arrange for part of this energy to be refined and little by little crystallized in us, so as to one day discover that a non-dependent structure has been established?

Saving this subtle energy-matter and fixing it in oneself is primarily a question of consciousness. Little by little, you feel more present, less inconsistent, more alive. This is a clue. In fact, all the efforts suggested to you here will help you save these foods, transform them into subtle matter and fix them within you.

What is necessary and what is not necessary on the way? Do you have to practice yoga breathing exercises? Do you have to repeat a mantra? Are rituals important or not? It is said that you can take the same voyage by train, by automobile or by airplane – all paths lead to the goal. But perhaps many of you have been troubled by this question: does the path that I am following lack something? Are there one or two common denominators or basic techniques which can be found on all paths?

Whether I was questioning Christian monks in France, Zen monks in the Orient, Tibetan and Sufi masters or Hindu sages, I invariably came across two common denominators to all spiritual paths. The first is what we call awareness. Awareness means consciously absorbing the different foods at the very moment when they inspire desire, fear, love or hate in us – all the usual emotions. Being aware lets us digest and assimilate these foods differently; the energy accumulated is therefore refined in a way that is not possible when we are identified with our emotions. "Keeping watch over your heart," "self-awareness," "being present to yourself and to God," "self-remembering," *dhikr* ("recollection" in Arab). Whatever the expressions, they point toward one and the same consciousness. All traditions keep coming back to the same leitmotif: "Watch and pray," "Be constantly aware," "Keep your heart with God and your hands at work," "Never forget your own Self," "Don't let yourself be distracted by the outside world, come back to yourself." Gregory the Great's talks on Saint Benedict, who was the founder of the Benedictine and Cistercian orders, put it eloquently: "Each time some overly-intense preoccupation pulls us out of ourselves, we remain ourselves and yet we are no longer with ourselves; we lose sight of ourselves and scatter ourselves in exterior things. But I noted that this venerable man [Saint Benedict] lived with himself for – being ever careful to watch over himself, keeping himself constantly in the presence of his Creator and ceaselessly examining himself – he did not let the sight of his soul become distracted outside."

The teachings of Buddha also stress the need to be mindful: "Those who are mindful already possess eternal life, those who are not mindful are already dead." A whole anthology could be compiled on this subject, drawing from all the great traditions. Living in a state of mindfulness is the first major difference with living in the ordinary way. Ordinarily, we do not realize how identified and confused we are; the subject is absorbed by the object with no distinction between the "spectator" and the "spectacle," between the witness and the phenomenon (the sensation, emotion or thought).

The second common denominator found in all traditions is linked to the first; if there is no trace of the first, there will be no trace of the second. It gives us a radically new attitude toward the mechanism of attraction and repulsion (I like/I don't like; I want/I don't want), in other words, our emotions. Some call it submitting to the will of God, others call it accepting what is , but whatever the words used, this attitude is completely out of the ordinary; it is radically different from the way the ordinary world teaches us to react. Emotion disappears when you understand the mechanism itself of emotion and stick to what is real. You will not find a single teaching which does not mention this. In Sanskrit, for example, you find the word "spots" or "stains" (*klesha*). But when you examine what these "spots" mean – hate, anger, greed, jealousy –

it becomes clear that they all denote emotions. This is the second common denominator.

Each time you consciously receive an impression or consciously experience a situation, you consume less energy and assimilate the energy received much better. Ordinarily, for every one hundred units of energy that nature gives you, you receive only ten. The others are squandered away, just as if you were constantly eating without ever managing to put on weight because your body neither retained nor fixed what it took in.

Receiving impressions while being self-aware, intensely conscious, means that, first of all, you consume less energy and assimilate more energy. Compared with the energy wasted by living in the ordinary way, you will thus save not twice but ten times more energy. The proportion seems enormous but no real inner transformation can take place unless a very great amount of energy is saved. In fact, each time you carry out this work on your emotions and – by being aware – you return to what is, each time you no longer let yourself be carried away either by a negative emotion or by a dependent happy emotion, you foster this inner alchemy, this transformation of energies.

First energy is saved, then it is transformed into more and more subtle matter and finally this subtle matter is fixed inside us. It is difficult to prove this process yet I agree with what Gurdjieff said because experience has shown me that it is true. We transform gross matter into fine matter when we no longer waste our energy in ordinary emotions, ordinary thoughts and the gross mechanisms they bring about. By being more aware and having less emotions, you stop losing what nature has put at your disposal. You receive more energy, consume less and transform the surplus by refining it. Much gross energy is needed to produce a small amount of fine energy in the same way as much wine must be distilled to produce a small amount of brandy.

The same laws apply on all levels – gross, subtle and causal. And one very interesting law is this: an increase in quantity produces a change in quality. If a metal is heated until it becomes red-hot, it gives off heat; if it is heated until it gets white-hot, it gives off light. If there is a quantitative increase in the degree of heat of a metal, it will get progressively hotter. Eventually a time will come when it will no longer produce heat but light. If you manage to increase the quantity of energy within yourself (energy which you save without wasting), a change in quality will come about. And instead of going through you and leaving nothing, this energy-matter becomes deposited in you, permeates your ordinary body and there develops a second body – called a subtle body – which one day crystallizes. Only the creation of this non-dependent inner body, which will encompass your entire manner of functioning (instinctive or motor, emotional, intellectual and sexual), can bring about your ultimate liberation.

～・・～

Although the way monks would describe this process is quite different from what I have been saying here, a monk's path also includes these two common denominators: awareness and work on the emotions. A monk who unremittingly practices awareness, who sees the will of God at work everywhere and has "purified his heart" through vigils and by keeping watch inwardly, also crystallizes an autonomous body. On all paths – that of the Zen, Tibetan or Trappist monk or that of the Vedantic meditator who dedicates himself to discriminating between the real and the unreal – if one's spiritual practice is conducted faithfully, the amorphous crowd always turns into a structured and hierarchically-organized people. And life no longer holds power over you.

In Japanese monasteries, there are two categories of monks: those who are still "under training" and the more advanced ones. A monk in training can still leave the monastery, quarrel with other monks, lose faith or decide that the abbot has made a mistake. But a monk who has gone beyond the training period is one who can be counted upon. Theoretically a master should not make mistakes!

In the great monasteries, responsabilities are given to a monk when it is certain that there is no longer any risk as far as he is concerned.

But one must not be too quick to assume that this crystallization has taken place. Perhaps it has just begun or is under progress. In chemistry, once there is saturation, the formation of crystals in a liquid takes place over a period of several hours, sometimes several days. In spiritual life, once a degree of saturation has been reached, the crystallization process itself takes a certain amount of time; it can still be interrupted and compromised. One must not rejoice too soon. It might take fifteen or twenty years to acquire an inner structure that will give you real mastery over yourself. But take heart. All the advice you have received and the effort you have put in, from your very first steps along a spiritual path, goes along with these two common denominators. Whether you swear only by Buddhist philosophy or by Thomist philosophy is secondary. What is essential is that this practice be carried out moment after moment during your own personal daily life.

In the past, I could not be free because I did not have this inner structure at my disposal. My lack of skill and understanding made me continue to have emotions without realizing it. And when I finally ended up in front of that yogi I had been seeking for so long, he considered that what I needed most was a structure. Whatever had I been doing in the Gurdjieff groups for twelve years, if he could strike me full in the face with such a revelation? It was that impossible-to-escape rigor of Swamiji, along with my practice of awareness and work on my emotions, that made it possible to create an inner structure. It is true that the *atman* or Buddha-Nature is the essence in each of us. But why have those who believe strongly that this is true not changed more? Some have even met Ramana Maharshi and stayed with him for up to ten years, hearing him repeat: "Only the Self exists, you are already free, all you need is to awaken." Why have they not awakened? Some who were fortunate enough to meditate every day in his presence for years still continued to be enslaved by their emotions. They were quick-tempered, jealous, criticizing each other and quarreling to the point where they no longer even spoke to one another. "One in a thousand seeks me, and out of a thousand who seek me, one finds me," says the Bhagavad Gita.

To put an end to this nightmare, you must build an inner structure over which the mind no longer has a hold, a structure which is free in all domains: intellectual, emotional and sexual. And the very fact that this structure is necessary shows that there is a tie between effort and result; it also helps you understand why certain spiritual practices succeed whereas others leave you at a virtual standstill. Do you persevere in your efforts or do you let the majority of occasions to progress escape you, day after day? If you have let yourself get carried away, you can come back to self-possession, to non-identification, to distinguishing between the spectator and the spectacle, to not letting the subject be absorbed by the object. There are so many expressions which are synonyms of awareness. Struggle so that you will not continue to be stuck in the mind, so that you will not take pleasure in negative emotions; come back to what is.

What is it that makes this Path one day bear lasting fruit? The conscious intake of foods. An increase in the quantity of accumulated gross energy can one day produce a change in quality. And each time that you change a negative attitude into an attitude of openness, you are taking a step in the direction of the crystallization we have been speaking about – of that you can be sure. A little of this subtle matter becomes deposited in you. But it will not saturate immediately and until there is crystallization, one can still be caught off-guard, even one who has much practice behind him. It is possible to have visibly progressed and then one fine day to abandon everything and start criticizing both the teachings and his guru. What happened? He simply did not follow through to the very end. But when crystallization comes about, there is no longer any risk. There can be no more relapses, no renewed counter-offensive from the mind – all that is over. The goal of your efforts, whether or not you realize it, is little by little to create this inner structure. Otherwise you will not obtain lasting results and you will be disappointed, discouraged: "I'm sinking back . . . I thought I had pulled through . . . I've fallen back onto my ordinary level . . . things aren't going the way I wanted them to . . ." The Way consists in freeing ourselves from certain laws to which we are subjected, laws studied in social sciences. When you follow the Way, you are escaping laws that govern jealousy, anger, aggressiveness, the fascination of love and the play of compensations. Certain laws, which used to apply to you, will little by little stop affecting you. Freedom awakens. Once this crystallisation takes place, a whole series of laws will stop pertaining to you once and for all.

Ramdas used to tell the following story. A man had bet that he could make Ramdas angry. For two hours, the man tried to make Ramdas "fly off the handle," as we say. Having lost his bet, the man sheepishly admitted everything to Ramdas and asked his forgiveness. The same story exists about Buddha in relation to someone who was showering him with insults. Buddha asked him: "If you offered me a present and I didn't take it, what would happen?" The man, a little surprised at this question after all his insults, answered: "I would be stuck with it." "Well then," added the Buddha, "just realize that I haven't taken any of your insults." A very simple yet remarkable little Catholic book with no esoteric pretentions, entitled *Trustful Surrender to Divine Providence: The Secret of Peace and Happiness*, relates another story in the same vein. During the first or second century after Jesus Christ, a Christian monk is beset by a group of pagans who make fun of him, saying: "Your God is a false God; your Jesus Christ never rose from the dead; your God can't perform any miracles." And the monk finally tells them: "Can't you see that at this very moment my God is performing a miracle? For three hours you have been trying to push me to the limit of my patience and you haven't succeeded in provoking the slightest emotion in me."

Both statements are true: on the one hand, we are already naked beneath our clothes; we are already the Self; there is no need to create it because it has been there for all eternity. But on the other hand, in this human life, how can we establish ourselves in the Self and become instruments of divine will? By creating an autonomous body, through awareness and through work on our emotions. It is these two themes that we constantly insist on here. Each time you come up against a situation, come back to what is, to non-duality within the moment itself, to being "one with" reality as it appears.

In the beginning, you see that you do not possess this structure and that you are always at the mercy of your emotions and your mind. You are not sure of yourself, feeling that there is a risk you are going to suffer again, to be afraid again. You become more or less advanced on the Way, having passed certain stages, but you know that this structure has not yet crystallized; it has only been outlined. You are not self-governing. And then one day, there is an about-face: you feel your autonomy. Something has really changed. You no longer function as you did before. The old mechanisms no longer work. Life orders you: "Be beside yourself with joy," and you no longer have to obey; life orders you: "Fall in love," and you no longer have to obey; life orders you: "Be furious," and you no longer have to obey. The mind has lost its power; you do not need to worry that there will be any relapses. You realize that you have stopped being a slave. The old ways with which you have struggled for so long have disappeared. The crystallization is completed.

3

FUNDAMENTAL ENERGY

TODAY I would like to speak further on the subject of sexual energy, yet what I have to say goes far beyond sexuality itself. It concerns all human beings, be they married, single or monks in a monastery. Swamiji used to say: *"Sex is fundamental energy manifested."* These words can be seen psychologically but they can also have a metaphysical sense, if one considers the bipolarity of opposites. It is for this reason that the Tantric sculptures or paintings of Tibet so often represent Tantric divinities mating; the male and the female are always procreators either in the natural sense or in a mystic sense, as we will see later. The famous circular diagram of yin and yang, with one black half and one white half interpenetrating each other, can also be seen as a sexual symbol. And in the *lingam* of Shiva emerging from the *yoni*, a cup which represents the female organ, the same symbolism is found once again.

Of course there are those who oversimplify such symbols, saying that sexuality plays such an important role in human life that man projects it into mythological or spiritual fantasies. But on the level of first principles – on the causal, ontological level – the universal manifestation itself is made up of this bipolarity and human sexuality is just one illustration of it. Sex is fundamental energy manifested, as long as you do not perceive the word "sex" only through the more or less pleasant memories you have (such as a few erotic pictures or pornographic films) or even in relation to a harmonious sex life. This statement takes on a much more vast meaning if you realize that sex and love are very often synonymous.

You may be familiar with Dante's famous verse: "Love which leads the world and the stars . . ." We could also say that love is fundamental energy manifested. (But what meaning will we then give to the word "love"?) And in everyday language, the term "making love" designates what is quite simply sexual mating – that is, the tendency to come together, to join, to commune.

All love, even of the highest kind, is a form of sexuality. I am speaking not in the name of Sigmund Freud, but of Swami Prajnanpad. You must remember that we were all born from two sex cells. Human beings do not come from the fusion of a bone cell and an epithelial cell! You were all born from an egg and a sperm. This cell proceeded to multiply and then to differentiate, to make up a complete human being. We originate from a particular form of universal energy which is human sexuality. And human sexuality includes not only the desire for union, but also sperm production in man and monthly ovulation in woman. Two sex cells fuse, and one day they give birth to a complete human being. This shows the priority of sexual energy, even though it subsequently branches out and specializes, becoming instinctive energy to make our lungs breathe and our heart beat, motor energy to perform voluntary movements, emotional energy to nourish the heart, intellectual energy for the brain and finally erotic energy itself.

Whatever position you may have towards sexuality – even if you are a monk or an ascetic living in total abstinence – Tibetan or Hindu tradition maintains that sexual energy is paramount. But what use do we make of this energy? This is where we see all the variety that exists in human nature. As we know, and as modern psychology has well demonstrated (although certain of Freud's ideas are disputable, others are unquestionable and can be proven valid by any honest specialist in social sciences), sexuality is present in all aspects of life, particularly in abnormalities and neuroses. A considerable number of psychologists and psychiatrists affirm that there is at least one sexual component in every neurosis. It cannot be otherwise, unless the word "sex" is taken only in its extremely restricted sense, and yet it must also be taken in its restricted (genital) sense.

In the manifested world, creation of any kind implies that two unite. (This is true for whatever level on which you take the word "creation.") And each time that two unite, it is a form of universal sexuality. Hindu tradition gives many images to illustrate this, but they are not all convincing for us. For example, it is only because you have an upper jaw and a lower jaw that you can speak. Or, can you make pottery with only one hand? A potter can make a pot on his wheel only if he uses his two hands – one hand inside the pot and the other outside. We may see these as rather elementary examples, but they have been authoritative ones for three thousand years.

On the metaphysical level, One cannot create. There can only be creation if there are two, that is if One has first divided. It is only by being dual that we can be creative. In the non-manifest state, there is nothing but the absolute silence of deep meditation or *samadhi*. The fact that two are necessary to create seems quite obvious in the procreation of a human being or an animal; in nature, procreation is an essential function of sexuality, although it is not the only one. Unless cells split in two to reproduce, there must be two: a father and a mother. The essential property of sexual energy is its creativity, both within duality and through the attempt of this duality to return to unity, that is, its attempt to bring together what is complementary or even what is apparently contradictory.

But it is not only in the procreation of a human being that sexuality is creative; it is *always* creative. A monk or a yogi, who never has sexual intercourse, nonetheless uses sexual energy to procreate the "new man" within himself. Human birth results from the sexual energy of a father and a mother. Spiritual birth, that new birth which comes about with the crystallization of the subtle body, is also produced by sexual energy. A yogi procreates himself in the form of a renewed and immortal being.

The procreation of a free and transformed inner being starts with fertilization from the outside: initiation takes place in a more or less solemn manner, through a look, a sound or a touch from a sage. If the "disciple" is not aborted – because the conditions of our lives are too trying and we forget what we felt during the moment of initiation – then that first shock becomes the start of a long process. A maturing process, similar to pregnancy, takes place. This new being grows inside, through spiritual practice, until there is saturation and the extremely fine matter which had little by little accumulated in us crystallizes, as explained in the preceding chapter. One day a birth takes place in us and we realize that we are no longer the same as we used to be: this "new man" that we have engendered no longer functions in the same way. It no longer reacts, is no longer affected and finds it quite easy to put the teachings into practice without having to carry on an unceasing struggle, punctuated by periods of forgetfulness and failure. But this inner procreation does not happen of its own accord. Nature does not take charge of it, like it takes charge of a baby's birth. Our active participation is demanded; in a way, we must become "the Creator's collaborators."

The new being that we have procreated inside is no longer subjected to the psychological laws which impose themselves upon the ordinary man, the "old man." Call this awakening, liberation, or illumination if you wish. There has been fertilization. As you know, initiation plays an essential role in all spiritual paths. Whether it is the shock of meeting a spiritual master or even that of coming across one of the sacred writings, one day your life changes. It is not exactly a birth . . . unless you consider birth as going back to when an egg is fertilized by a sperm. In any case, this is the birth of the disciple in us, even if it is not the birth of the new man.

Even a yogi who is faithful to Pantanjali's *Yoga-Sutras* and does not actually have any erotic life (as opposed to other paths) – even he cannot be the creator of this new man unless there are "two" in him. What I am now going to tell you does not only apply to monks who have a totally internalized sex life. It also applies to you – even though all of you (or almost all) are destined to lead a particular sex life.

～ ‧ ‧ ⁓

You carry both male and female qualities within you. Female qualities are ones of welcoming and receptivity, just as the vagina welcomes the penis and the uterus welcomes the sperm. Reflection and meditation are also regarded as female, because they are connected to what happens during pregnancy – a inner maturing. In contrast, the so-called male qualities concern outside action: giving, emitting, promoting. No one can claim that these statements are based on a sexual obsession, a projection of the penis and the female sex onto everything, as was unjustly said of Sigmund Freud. There is both a man and a woman in all of us. Nothing in that statement implies male superiority, female inferiority or sexism. In the book *Toward the Fullness of Life*, I tried to show how female values are today tragically forgotten. (And I weigh my words.) Every woman possesses in herself the wealth of male qualities, and every man has the wealth of female values within him; the path of yoga in its pure state, is actually that of uniting the male and the female inside us. These male and female possibilities, once unified and harmonized, procreate the new man in the evangelical sense of the word. A free man can thus become an instrument of what each situation demands or of the will of God. Unlike an un-regenerated man, he is no longer a machine reacting to outside appeals.

These male and female qualities, which form the basis of sexual bipolarity, are not equally developed in all of us – men or women. To a certain degree, one can say that female values predominate in women and male values in men. I am not speaking now about homosexuality; that is a separate case. Let me simply say in passing that my conviction – as opposed to that of the Catholic Church – is that homosexuality is not an invalidating and implacable hindrance on one's spiritual path.

Every human being, whether or not he or she has a sex life, must experience a particular aspect of bipolarity, namely, the uniting of his or her own male and female components. The ideas I am sharing with you are not interesting from a merely ontological point of view; they can be applied practically and concretely. Some men are quite open to female values. They are capable of listening, of letting things mature in them, of being silent, welcoming and receptive to divine grace. Spirituality implies being open; it is largely female. In Brindavan, all pious men consider themselves female and it is said that Krishna is the only man there. All the others – even bearded, muscular, learned men – are considered *gopis* (shepherdesses wholeheartedly in love with the enrapturing Krishna).

Since female characteristics are more or less atrophied from the outset, they must be developed. But you will not be able to procreate the sage in yourself if you only have female aspects of openness and receptivity. Acting, projecting and externalizing are also important values on the Way. You must clearly see the necessity of both sides.

A woman may have strong male traits, sometimes even to the detriment of her femininity. A man or woman's astrological chart can provide interesting information in this regard, according to how the planets are distributed among the male and female signs. (Water and earth signs are female; air and fire signs are male.) For example, Aries, with its impulsive and primary aspects, is typically male. It charges. In past times, herds of rams were actually used to break down gates. If Aries plays a significant role in a woman's chart, she must accept the fact that she has a pronounced male component. How will she harmonize that with what is called femininity? Some men's charts likewise reveal predominant female characteristics, making it necessary for them to put in particular effort to develop their male assertiveness.

You realize therefore how important your male and female components are, be you a man or a woman. But to procreate this new man, you must reach a level of being which is considerably free of the elements of your chart. (I am not saying absolutely free.) The saying, based on ignorance or prejudice, that declares "One cannot change one's nature" is not true. The very nature of man is just that: the capacity to change. Of course you cannot change a Japanese into a Senegalese, nor will you completely modify your being. There will always be a certain style. But on this path, you must develop and harmonize all your potentials. If your chart helps you understand yourself better then that understanding should be accompanied by the decision to change your nature since that is where man's dignity lies – just as the dignity of a caterpillar lies in its changing into a butterfly. So we accept to balance ourselves and thus to develop in ourselves that part which as yet remains atrophied. The male and female are designated by Tibetans as being the father and mother in us (*yab – youm*) who procreate the liberated man, the one who has rediscovered his original image.

I often say that we have nothing to create: we have only to discover, just as we are already naked beneath our clothes. This may seem to contradict what I am saying today about the need to procreate. These two approaches are not incompatible. As they say in India, they are just two ways of looking at things or two angles of vision (*darshana* in Sanskrit, a key word in Hindu logic). From one point of view, it is true that we already are the Buddha-Nature or brahman or atman but only a re-generated man can establish himself in brahman. And it is precisely in order to create this "twice-born" man that effort is necessary on the different paths. These words concern your sexuality on its most concrete level (whether you are impotent, frigid or a great lover) at the same time as they apply to your spiritual life on its highest level.

Every *sadhana* has a double aspect: an active aspect and a purely receptive aspect of non-action. It is true that certain *sadhanas* are largely female while others are mostly male, yet they can all lead to the goal. When the Gospels say, "The violent will seize the Kingdom of Heaven by force," this applies to the male aspect of spiritual practice. Non-action and inner silence represent the female aspect. There is a balance to be found between these two approaches.

If you are too active in your practice, the ego manages to get something out of it. Consequently, the idea of a battle sometimes becomes the basis for one's *sadhana*. It is true that Mohammed spoke of the Great Holy War but that is exactly what makes up the ego – fighting. Once the ego no longer finds an adversary, then the ego is no more. From birth, what characterizes the ego is *being against*. It is born, grows up and develops, provided that it can resist something. It is formed in a small child as soon as he or she starts to oppose Mom and Dad. The anal stage, for example, called the aggressive stage, represents a phase of ego formation in which the child stands up to Mom. And since adults opposed you, the outside influences or traumatic memories you have introjected make you condemn a part of yourself. Some, for whom these mechanisms are not clear, use either an ideal which they sincerely believe to be spiritual or else yoga and concentration techniques in order to muzzle that part of themselves that they refuse. And although they are convinced that they are fighting against their weaknesses, they are actually mutilating the life within themselves and consequently, their own sexuality.

If you stop denying one important aspect of yourself, then a whole pillar of your ego collapses. This is why the word yes is the absolute weapon against the ego. This is not only true for disciples of a Hindu or Tibetan master, any psychologist who has studied the genesis of the ego in childhood will agree. Take care that the active part of your *sadhana* does not strengthen your ego, which can thus continue its everlasting struggle by deciding "I'm going to fight against this chain of thoughts, I will reduce them to silence; they bother me in my meditation, I'll defeat them by concentrating on my breathing. We'll see who is the stronger."

I do not deny the fact that every *sadhana* includes a certain struggle. The word "concentration" in Patanjali's yoga definitely implies a battle against parasite thoughts. This is a male *sadhana*. But although it is right for the disciple to find joy in his progress, it is also necessary to watch out for the subtle trap which lies in wait for all spiritual seekers. This trap consists in reinforcing the ego and developing a superego with a halo of spirituality. If, for example, you acquire certain powers after successfully applying yourself to exercises on the "hara" or on body consciousness, you may go astray, thinking: "Now I'm going to be better than others because I'll be centered and well-structured, with a strong focal point in the lower abdomen." In fact, you are quite simply opposing one aspect or another of yourself – very often without intending to do so – as a result of unconscious reactions.

If indeed almost all neuroses are found to have a sexual component, it is due to the fact that human beings too often fight against their own sexuality, in a more or less twisted manner. And we fight it because we are afraid. Take a humble look at how this statement applies to you. Let me repeat that sexual energy is the manifestation of the fundamental energy from which you were born. If yin and yang are united in perfect balance, there is no manifestation, no creation. It is your sexual force alone that will make you the creator of a structured and awakened inner being . . . or else it will quite simply make you creative. But the majority of human beings reject some part of themselves. Love is always at the root of this denied part – as is hate, which is the inverse of love. The same man who wrote "I love you, I love you, I love you" can fire a gunshot at the object of his passion. "I loved her too much . . . I couldn't stand seeing her leave with another man. . . I killed her, your honor."

Mechanical reactions show either this immense fusionary force or the distortion of this force, which turns into hate and aggressiveness. All drives are forms of fundamental energy. And fundamental energy is the same in a Don Juan as in a monk, except that it is used differently. It is love which leads the mountain climber to the peaks and the navigator to the seas. When someone enters into conflict with some aspect of himself, it is always ultimately a conflict with his sexual force. And certain men and women, even though they like making love, remain boxed into an impoverished and limited sexuality because they are afraid of their own vital force.

Every path of initiation therefore includes a certain degree of combativeness but the female portion in spirituality is far more important. Whether you are man or woman, you will only become a sage by letting the spiritual part in yourself bloom, that is, the female side of receptivity, silence, contemplation and self-giving. Mystic vocabulary often uses expressions that are reserved to the sexual domain. Just as we say a man "takes a woman," so too is it said that God takes possession of a soul. And for God to take possession of us, we must become female; we must let ourselves be penetrated and impregnated by the divine. Surrender and letting-go are fundamental elements in spirituality.

You cannot use yoga and self-awareness exercises to help you fight and scheme better in life, armed with a sword on the one side and a shield on the other. Do not deceive yourself. In Japan, the culmination of martial arts consists in "never conquering but in never being conquered either." The great accomplishment for a master of martial art is to die in his bed, because he has only to appear for peace to reign. In fact most Japanese words designating the martial arts actually signify arts of peace. Do not let the martial aspect, which is so fascinating for us modern Westerners, mislead you. Peace is greater than combat.

The idea that the *sadhana* is both male and female is closely akin to two very important notions in Swamiji's vocabulary: *"the way of peace and the way of power."* The male attitude leads to power – and power over oneself or self-possession definitely has its place. But the way of power – or that of "powers" in the plural, when it is only *siddhis* (miraculous powers) that are sought – has its limits. The ultimate mystic way is the way of "peace which passes all understanding." Ramana Maharshi apparently possessed no powers. He was neither deputy nor minister; he had no financial means; he was content just to exist and to be radiant.

It is true that it is essential to acquire real power over oneself. You cannot tolerate to go on indefinitely, year after year, being the plaything of your thoughts and impulses, going around in circles within the same mechanisms, the same childishness and the same weakness. If a warrior arises in you, Congratulations! . . . as long as you remain open to silence and receptivity. Be strong, win battles, but if there is a part of yourself with which you are not at peace, be careful not to condemn it in the name of the *sadhana*. If so, you will be done for. If you are not first reconciled with your ambition, your vanity, your violence, your aggressiveness and your sexuality even in its most animal aspects, then the *sadhana,* because of its fighting nature, may become an instrument of your neurosis.

So you must undertake a balanced *sadhana,* otherwise you will never be free. Your entire capacity to fight – to "pitch into" things as we say, both concretely and figuratively – is a male manifestation of the sexual energy in you; this capacity has its place in the process of transformation toward opening up, letting-go and self-giving. If a woman presses her thighs and her knees together, if her vagina shrinks back, how can she be penetrated? *"What does nature say?"* asked Swamiji. A female attitude is essential because is it not after all a woman who carries a baby for nine months? A woman is impregnated but she is the one who makes the baby; in procreation, her role is more important than that of the man. Both provide a cell at the start, but the work of gestation then falls to the woman. In the same way, in generating an inner being (and this is the real goal of spirituality, whether you are a man or a woman), the role of the woman in you takes precedence over that of the man in you.

᠁

The birth of the new man in oneself corresponds largely to what I have called the crystallization of the subtle body; this latter then ceases to be amorphous and formless. But at the same time, you are destined to express yourself and to act. Birds sing, peacocks spread their tails, trees produce flowers and fruit. In order to feel that you are really in harmony with the universe, in order to become fully a man or a woman, you must be creative. The spiritual teachings say that man becomes God's collaborator and perfects creation.

Of course I cannot agree with some of the absurd things that have been written on this subject, such as: "No one can deny that God caused the brontosaurus and the diplodocus to become extinct, so when modern man destroys different animal species, he is doing so as the collaborator of God who intends to make lions, tigers and elephants become extinct, just as he did the brontosaurus." In brief: go ahead, ransack nature, no ecology, let not a single elephant nor a single tiger survive on the face of the planet. Such is the result of this insidious line of reasoning. Man is said to be God's collaborator in creation, but unfortunately a misunderstanding of this by the Christianity of our time has led to abuses which are greatly condemned today. And it sends shivers down one's spine to imagine that these abuses could lead to the destruction of our planet.

If you are a creator, you are playing your role as a human being. But the majority of human beings are not very creative. They cannot even renew themselves . . . they imitate, plagiarize and re-use. For one scenario with a truly original idea, you will find fifty scenarios which use the same ingredients again and again. And even if you are not what is actually called a creator (such as a stage designer, movie director, writer, potter or ceramic artist), you must be creative in a subtle manner so that your entire life will become a permanent creation. Every evening, a dancer creates his performance before the eyes of his public: his creation is born when he comes on stage; it dies when he goes back into the wings.

Think about that word. How can you become creative everywhere, in all domains and on all levels, instead of leading a life which is just a reproduction, an imitation from the outside, a submission to "what is done and what is not done" with no originality. Your behavior is repetitive, and repetition is the characteristic of neurosis. Your behavior copies, either by direct imitation or by negative imitation, that is, by doing the opposite of one's inner engraved patterns. And if you are a slave to certain idiotic but very cruel laws decreed by your mind, then you are no longer capable of renewing yourself. The freer you are, the more natural, spontaneous and original your life will be . . . *"a festival of newness"* to use the words of Swamiji.

For there to be fertility, there must be two. So it is really *in yourself* that you must work out the man-woman balance, even if this inner harmony plays an exclusive role only in paths which completely eliminate sexual intercourse and which therefore primarily entail an aspect of struggle with oneself. There are however other paths, ones said to be "of the world," which allot a place to eroticism. In Tibet, the two paths coexist. You have all heard of *Tantra* . . . although, alas, in an often degenerate form. In Tantra, sexuality is considered sacred. But certain Tantric monks – gelukpas and the Dalai Lama, for example – do not have any sex life.

The principle of Tantra, either Tibetan or Hindu, is never to be against anything. No matter what, a human life can only be right if it is founded on a massive "yes" to sexuality. A monk whose monastic vocation is based on a refusal of sexuality, sabotages his life as a monk. Normally, a monk is full of sexual energy when he enters a monastery. Ancient texts are eloquent on this, as illustrated by the question formerly asked of those who wanted to enter a monastery: "So you want to live in chastity, do you have good erections?" It is only after full responsibility is taken for one's sexuality that it can be used spiritually. Unfortunately, this is not the case for many Westerners.

Tantric meditations, which are based on awareness instead of on efforts to concentrate on a given theme, are of a female nature. The flow of ideas and daydreams is welcomed without denial, but the devotee does not identify with them; instead he lets them pass on. Dudjom Rinpoche told me: "Hinayana uses concentration to struggle against enemies and obstacles whereas in mahayana, we do not dread these because we know the antidote, *shunyata*, the belief in the emptiness and unreality of all phenomena. But in *tantrayana*, the devotee does not fear poisons (contrary to the *hinayanist* who must lower his eyes so as not to be troubled by a woman) because he knows how to digest poisons." Swamiji often cited a proverb to me: *"One man's food is another man's poison."* Any active substance acts either as medicine or as poison. We have been poisoned on a psychological level because we have been taught to condemn certain aspects of our own truth, like a child's tantrums when he cannot get the better of a toy or other drives which come out in their raw state during early childhood. So a child develops the habit of being in conflict with his own vital impulses, his fundamental life force, what Freud called the "libido," which is at work everywhere. It is important to approach this topic and to hear the word "sexuality" in a completely new way and from a completely new viewpoint. Drop all that tarnishes or condemns sexuality, like bad memories that link masturbation with shame or the awkwardness you felt with the opposite sex when you were young. The intelligence of the heart can convince us to leave behind these falsified and neurotic images for a metaphysical understanding which, little by little, will counterbalance the imprints of the past, create what I call "counter-*samskaras*" and move from the intellect down into feeling.

For those with a so-called normal sex life, there is one more point to understand. Sexual intercourse is procreative, eventually of a child but also of the new man and the new woman in each of the partners. This truth is completely lost from sight in the course of life, even though marriage remains a sacrament in all traditions. Far Eastern literature emphasizes the union of yin and yang – in sex too. Chinese, Japanese and Hindu treatises are genuine sex manuals, transcribing what the erotic sculptures of the Khajuraho temples transmit visually: the mystical aspect of sexual mating.

This yin-yang union takes place when we balance our male and female potentialities. It takes place within a monk, hermit or yogi who may not even cross paths with a single woman for twenty years, and it takes place in a sex life which is both fulfilling and relaxed, because of the woman's openness to the yang values of the man and the man's openness to the yin values of the woman. There is a communion that takes place, either through contact – with or without penetration – or through simple physical closeness, making it possible to feel the other's vibrations and to exchange energies. Each of the partners takes a share in this procreation, as long as no inhibition, refusal or fear (in other words, no neurosis) compromises the play of nature in us. One of the ways to procreate the "integral man" or the "integral woman" in oneself consists in being two *outwardly,* that is, by forming a couple in which the woman assimilates the yang emanations of the man, and the man, the yin emanations of the woman. It is also for this reason (not just for ordinary psychological ones) that a man and a woman share the same bed. During sleep, a certain impregnation takes place on the subtle level. If the spouses are truly open to each other, an energy radiates which is not the same in the man and in the woman and they complement each other.

To situate yourself in the right manner, ask yourself with ease and honesty what trauma, what distortions, what repressions have made you more or less inhibited. There are many ways of no longer being sexually normal. Even in an apparently satisfactory sex life, you can be sexually limited if you remain confined to purely genital relaxation because this will never lead you to a transcendental level. The sex life of one who is emotionally free is always transcendent. The Latin phrase: "Man is a sad animal after coitus" only applies to human beings who are closed to spiritual realities and whose sexuality does not open out onto this creativity. After the sex act or after physical closeness which does not include the sex act itself, one should not feel tired or disappointed – or guilty – but rather renewed. In Swamiji's own words: first be *normal,* because by being perfectly normal you will naturally go toward the *supranormal*. The sex act aids inner growth because it regenerates. I have read much on this subject – by psychologists, sexologists and psychoanalysts – and for twenty years I have been listening to what has been confided in me by men and women whose sex life was not normal, in the sense Swamiji gave to the word. It was therefore not a "re-creation" and did not make them creative.

Swamiji reminded me many times that the whole is greater than the sum of its parts. He gave me a simple example, one that is easy to understand for someone with no scientific background. *"If you take five strands of rope, each with a carrying capacity of one kilo, and weave them together in a certain way, the woven rope will carry seven or eight kilos instead of five."* This law applies to a real couple, be it a durable one or an occasional one. When one plus one unite, two is greater than one plus one. New creative possibilities thus come to light, ones which directly concern your inner growth. But I wish to repeat that this will only happen if there is nothing in your conscious or unconscious to thwart this natural blossoming forth.

Of course all of this has a realistic aspect yet it is also based on a spiritual teaching. Tantrism cannot be reduced to the way certain yoga teachers use it – to seduce their prettiest students. Tantra implies perfect acceptance, and thereby the prevalence of the female aspect, which opens completely to the sexual urge – either in its direct expression or in a transposed form – and thus leads to love. Sex has both human and spiritual value. Love is the universal law. India showed this very well by offering a progressive path in which sexuality first has full importance, until the time comes when sex passes into the background because a communion other than genital exchange becomes possible between the man and the woman.

The powerful force which leads the universe is none other than love. Two bodies unite – that is love; two souls fuse – that is love; two minds commune – that is love; a heart goes toward another –

that is love. For sex to be a form of love and so that the expression "making love" will not be a mockery, sex must be experienced without restriction and without pre-conceived ideas, and there must be love at least here and now. What does this mean? After all, the word "love" has a multitude of meanings and in French, as well as in English, this same word is used to designate greed, passion, infatuation and other particularly twisted forms of selfishness . . .

There is love only if one's whole being participates, if only for the moment itself. Living the present moment is the keystone to any kind of intense life and to any kind of spirituality, but especially to sexuality which is right, here and now, second after second, without past and without future, with total, intellectual, emotional and physical involvement. Most times, human beings are incapable of this. They see such total involvement in the present moment as being particularly unattainable in a relationship with no tomorrow, even though this is the case in certain sacred ritualistic, transitory unions. I cannot go into the particular case of each human being and his or her sex life, but it is possible for love to exist at least at the given moment, in the fullness of the here and now, even during sex which is not founded on the sacrament of marriage or on a lasting union. There are many examples of this in the history of various forms of spirituality: the partners will never see each other again so that there will be no ordinary attachment and so that there can be complete reunification, similar to what happens during a rewarding meditation in which head, heart and body are reunited in momentary but total self-giving. Indeed, this total involvement in the present moment could take place even in what we call chance encounters. But in fact, it never does because we are afraid to give ourselves, because we are not unified, because we do not know ourselves and therefore cannot count on ourselves and because we do not dare to play the game.

Giving oneself involves a freedom which is not immediately available to human beings. A yogi tries to belong to himself so that he will be able to give himself. This gift of oneself proves easier if one has the help of a union based on trust and future commitment, like in a consecrated marriage. But real surrender in sex is not when a man and woman give themselves for life or for eternity in front of a priest; it happens second after second, for it is only the perfection of the present moment that puts us into contact with the vertical dimension of the eternal present or eternity. When there is no longer either past or future, when there exists nothing but an endless present, then this religious vertical dimension reveals itself and we discover the metaphysical aspect of existence. And sex helps human beings – even if they are not yet very advanced yogis – to concentrate here and now, in the present moment, and thereby to enter timelessness.

For this, understanding is needed. On the path that I propose, everything starts with understanding. One pure instant opens out onto eternity. But ordinarily we experience sex on a background of greed; this makes us always live the present moment in relation to the moment which is to follow, straining toward a goal. Actually, sex should be experienced not only without relation to the past (the nightmare of the past which warps, tarnishes, sullies and inhibits our possibilities) but without relation to the future (not even a future that is a half-hour or one minute from now). The sexual experience then becomes a reunification in which we can be sustained by the very force of sexual energy, the fundamental energy of which intellectual, emotional and physical energy are only ramifications.

If the above three differentiated functions are "put under the same yoke" – that is, if they are in yoga – there results an aware-ness of being and of being alive that is freer and more intense, accompanied by an unaccustomed feeling of ease, simplicity and spontaneity.

Sex is a precious help toward becoming whole again. Since you are not now great meditators able to enter into *samadhi* at will, you need help at the beginning of the way. By perfecting the here and now, by reuniting the whole of your being and by simultaneously giving and receiving, your male and female aspects will be in balance or harmony. Each partner gives and each partner receives; indeed, as one of the great Upanishads says: "they fulfill each other's desire." This mutual exchange produces a desireless state, a moment of plenitude and thereby a creative, re-creating, state. It is a recreation which gives each partner the possibility to love – and this is actually a momentary effacement of the ego.

But when the sex act is based on judgement and unconscious condemnation, the experience is falsified even if the woman has an orgasm and the man a certain pleasure in ejaculation. However if the ego is momentarily effaced, the culmination of the sex act is always a beginning instead of an end. Even though the feeling of breaking off, almost a sadness, is generally more pronounced in the man, in some women the abnormal element manifests itself in a negative reaction after they have been carried away by the sex drive. Under normal conditions, the result of the sex act, which we commonly call orgasm, is far from a conclusion; it is like a door which opens onto another world. Some human beings have had this kind of experience that emerged onto a state of grace although they had never even heard of spirituality – indeed you might say it happened while they were "making it" (and I am purposely using a cavalier expression). I have heard various descriptions of sexual intercourse which resemble *samadhi*.

You can efface the ego here and now by completely accepting universal energy in yourself and submitting to it. By letting yourself melt into sensation and daring to give your sensations enormous importance. There is more to life than the intellect. Dare to become somewhat animal. Although it is experienced from moment to moment, this dynamism is a continuity, an ongoing process, a drive. All is movement in life; nothing remains fixed. Even in the most motionless meditation, blood and prana continue to circulate.

Swamiji said: *"There is only giving, only receiving."* The ego is effaced through non-dualistic action. We can practice being one with our breathing so that only conscious breath remains – one, not two; in the same way, if a man kisses a woman there is only kissing. What Swamiji explained to me is not valid only for sex, but it is easier to put into practice in that domain. Another example Swamiji gave me was this: "not *I look at the tree*, but *the tree is being looked at.*" If the tree is being looked at, I no longer see *my* tree, in relation to my previous history, my cultural context and my unconscious. Each time I look at an oak, if I see it in relation to the really splendid one that grew in my grandfather's garden, I no longer see the tree itself, but instead keep seeing my grandfather's tree. But if the tree is looked at, I no longer see the oak of my grandfather's garden, instead I see the oak which is there in front of me.

This experience can be applied to life in general, but it takes a particular place in sex where it includes all the levels of one's being: the physical and emotional as well as the mental; all the *koshas* are involved and all five senses take part. It is no longer "I am caressing this woman" but rather "this woman is being caressed." Then I myself, as an individualized ego, disappear. I enter into contact with the very movement of life. Sexual energy had no need of you to create an embryo when you were no bigger than an insect inside your mother. Not "I" am caressing this woman, this woman is being caressed; there is only kissing . . . there is only caressing. This is a real opportunity for effacing the ego.

~ · ~

In the meditation exercises that we do here, do not ever be surprised at how much importance is given to developing an awareness of the lower abdomen (seat of the *hara*) or the sacrum (seat of the sleeping *kundalini*), and even the whole lower part of the body, including the anus and the genital organs. For a doctor, the sex center is located neither in the ovaries nor in the testicles; it is somewhere in the brain. Yet ancient knowledge lists other bodily centers which you have all heard referred to as chakras. Exerting a light push on the *hara* while exhaling not only accumulates energy in the *hara* but also accumulates prana in the genital organs.

This technique can be used to stay young – as in the Taoist tradition – because the procreative force is located in the lower abdomen. The fine energy of prana accumulates in this part of your system and you feel your lower abdomen completely regenerated, more alive and more vibrant (even if there is no erection, for the man).

Sometimes spiritual practices increase the intensity of what psychoanalysts call the "libido." Monks and nuns know what sexual storms are, quite simply because certain concentration exercises intensify one's energy and this latter is no longer dispersed in daydreams. Turning inward and contemplation – even in ways other than the *hara* practices – inevitably produce an increase in sexual energy because, in fact, sexual energy is quite simply energy itself. Some dedicate themselves to a religious path and are disturbed to find themselves becoming almost obsessed. This should not worry you: if unusual things happen and you remain a pure witness, they will very quickly disappear as long as you do not deny them. Accept once and for all that there is nothing indecent, nothing "Tantric" (in the Western sense of the word), in accumulating energy in the lower abdomen. All is pure for those who have a pure heart – even if this has become quite difficult for us.

It is absolutely normal to feel, without reticence, a force or energy accumulating "below the belt" as the expression goes. Just take a look at the scornful connotation that expression has. Fucking and stuffing oneself, they're not at all spiritual! The *hara* is located below the belt; for a yogi the seat of the kundalini is located below the belt; sexuality, the most precious energy, which is referred to in mystic texts as that which evokes the highest spiritual accomplishments, also originates below the belt. In India, God is described as being a man and a woman so tenderly enlaced that each no longer knows who is the man and who is the woman. This also describes a trinity: a man, a woman and love. The most sacred activity of all is sex. That it has been greatly profaned, I agree. But we must come back to an understanding of its true dimension.

It is true that the *hara* practice can have positive repercussions on one's sex life. I still remember Sensei Deshimaru, whom I deeply loved and respected, saying in his bad French as he used his arm in a gesture which was both vulgar and explicit to imitate the male sex: "Zazen, zazen, oh . . . la madame she is happy!" His was without a doubt the crude way of a Zen master. Yet Zen monks are not what are known as Tantric monks, with sexual partners, *shaktis* or *dakinis* in their monastery. They therefore use this manifested fundamental energy for their inner growth. If you have no sex life because the conditions of your life do not allow you to have a partner, do not worry; these exercises will not increase your libido to the point where it will become torture not to be able to make love.

I am speaking crudely in order not to pretend to deny the problems you face. As Rajneesh said: "People come to see me under the pretext that they are seeking God; if they were seeking God, there would be no problem – but actually, they come to see me because they are sexually frustrated and that is much more difficult to solve." Obviously this influx of vitality should not just be considered as energy which will force you to have a sex life but rather as energy which is absolutely necessary for your development, even if circumstances have condemned you to celibacy. It is the Life within you that is concerned. From a certain point onward, an increase in quantity brings about a change in quality. Sexual energy is the real energy of Love. . . not only of the love that is an unstable emotion springing from sentimentality and weakness but of real, profound and immutable love, the love of a saint for his fellow man.

But let there be no misunderstanding on this point: the goal of meditation exercises is not to make you more sexually potent but rather to produce fine energy in you. Sexual energy is very fine energy; that is a fact which is known and taught throughout Asia. But we have reduced sex to the rank of an animal-like activity; we have slandered, degraded and sullied it through the wrong functionings of our mind. Yet it is sexual energy which makes transmutation possible.

Whether you have a sex life or whether the circumstances of your life condemn you not to have one, do not be worried. Take your destiny as it is today and be at peace with it. But I am asking each of you to reflect on all this with an open heart in the goal of reconciling yourselves with sexual energy. And be particularly careful of any mental reservations based on the fact that in practices dealing with what is "below the belt," namely the *hara*, your sexual force is implicated.

For my own part, I had received a very religious upbringing where everything was imagined as being impure. There was no salvation for someone who made love outside marriage and both the man and the woman were supposed to be virgins when they got married. Otherwise they were betraying the Christian ideal. The Gurdjieff groups convinced me that sexual relations, far from being a sin, could be a very fine "food of impression." I therefore ended up feeling that I was quite normal sexually and yet there was still something lacking. It was Asia that made me discover the sacred dimension of the sexual force, no matter how it is used.

To a man, nothing seems more terrible than the idea of being castrated. But that is exactly what happens to a human being who cuts himself off from his own vital force and his capacity to love. There is something that deserves to be insisted upon, something that looks paradoxical at first: sexual force is the force of mystical love. If you are not at peace with your sexuality – even if you are in love – your love will not reach the spiritual level. A yogi or a monk from Mount Athos, who will never take a woman in his arms, nonetheless uses sexual energy to carry out his spiritual practice. And if you refuse this energy in yourself, simply because you consider it to be exciting, granted, but animal-like, then you are condemning yourself to a wasted life. All that people have entrusted in me has shown me what suffering this natural function can cause, for both men and women, when it has been distorted, deviated and perverted.

4

SEX AND THE HEART

WHETHER you admit it or whether you deny it, sex is not only the origin of every human existence but, in either a rough or spiritualized state, it continues to be the basic drive in everyone's life. This is not just a Freudian statement; much of mystic or metaphysical symbolism portrays the same thing.

If you go by appearances, fate seems unjust. It gives certain men or women a fulfilling sex life while others experience nothing but frustration. Sexuality may thus be a painful subject for some, but you cannot follow a spiritual path worthy of the name by closing your eyes, running away and cheating. At the same time, I would like to insist on the fact that no situation is ever hopeless on the path of inner freedom – that would be too cruel. In life, there can be hopeless situations . . . for example, there is no doubt that being forced to file a petition for bankruptcy is disastrous from a professional point of view. But on the Way, there is no such thing as a hopeless situation . . . there are just people who lose hope in a situation. Think of water . . . it always manages to pass! It filters through sand, goes around rocks and flows along until it reaches a stream; the stream joins a river and the river merges into the ocean. I am saying this for those of you to whom existence has not granted a rich sex life. Yet through all the ups and downs of your sex life, it is necessary to see that the sexual function (or what Gurdjieff calls the sex center) is a definite reality. It is in fact a vast reality, no matter what form each person's sexual energy may take.

How is it possible to regain childlike spontaneity in the sex act itself? Spontaneity is a prevailing theme in universal spirituality, not just in Christianity. "Unless you become like little children, you cannot enter the Kingdom of Heaven." A sage is childlike, but this in no way means that he or she is childish. A child – who has no past, no references and no value judgements – lives, expresses himself and plays freely. But we adults have more or less (and unfortunately, in general, it tends to be more, rather than less) lost such spontaneity. This childlike simplicity must be rediscovered. But a child's games do not include the dimension that underlies sex. Without being out-of-balance with yourself in one way or another, you cannot reduce sexuality to nothing more than an enjoyable pastime; it is much more than that. So there are two aspects which must be considered: simplicity and grandeur.

Since we have lost the naturalness we knew as a child and have been influenced by all sorts of judgements and opinions, it can be helpful to counterbalance our upbringing with other ideas. These ideas must be strong, convincing and completely different; in particular, they must underline the spiritual and even the mystic value of sexuality. Let this certainty sink deeper and deeper inside you. As a help, I would like to go over some truths which are very well described in the book *In Search of the Miraculous*, provided you read it attentively without overlooking anything. I am even going to use the same terminology as that book since a good part of my fifteen-year spiritual search consisted in verifying if what I had understood from the Gurdjieff teachings was both true and universal.

We are made up of a more or less lucid intellectual center, as well as an emotional center encumbered with emotions which, once purified, will become what Gurdjieff calls the higher emotional center. (I do not feel that the word "emotion" is a well-chosen one here.) We also have a physical center – that of the sensations we perceive – composed of a moving side (which is learned), plus an instinctive side (which is not learned). A child is not taught to suckle, much less to make his heart beat and his lungs breathe. And finally, we have a sex center.

Now each center functions by using a relatively gross or fine energy proper to itself. We assimilate the energy nature gives us and this energy enables a subtle body to crystallize in us, thus creating an autonomous inner structure which functions on a level of quality independent of ordinary mechanisms. Our subtle body allows us to enter into contact with the highest levels of reality, higher states of consciousness and divine feelings. The energy proper to the sex center itself has a very high level of quality. This is something we have completely forgotten because, in our Judeo-Christian civilization, we have developed the attitude that while sex is a pleasure it is also a purely profane act . . . not to say a spiritual weakness. Even today, this suspicion with regard to sex in relation to the higher values has not disappeared. There are definitely those who have a certain degenerate attitude towards their love life but this has nothing to do with sex itself, as nature created it.

The sex act cannot be reduced to a beastlike function, even though man also is an animal, a mammal; this too must be taken into account. As the saying goes: if you betray the earth in yourself, you will never attain the heaven in yourself. (*"Qui veut faire l'ange fait la bête."*) The energy of the sex center vibrates at the same degree of intensity as the energy which inspires the finest of feelings: peace, serenity, love, bliss, all the inner states which make the heart expand. This is why there are so many connections between sex and mysticism (all degenerations aside for the time being). And it is why abstinence – when rightly used by those qualified to practice it, who know the right methods for transmuting energy – can produce such great spiritual results. The reason why erotic vocabulary is so often used in mysticism is that the same fine level of energy exists both in mysticism and in a fulfilling sex life. Such vocabulary is found even in the great classic Upanishads (the Brihadaranyaka and Chandogya), not just in the Tantric Upanishads where the word *maithuna* (mating) describes certain metaphysical or theological realities. The Canticle of Canticles, which no one has ever dared abolish from the Old Testament, is another example of this. And even in popular speech, the word "ecstasy" or the expression "seventh heaven" is sometimes used for orgasm. But just what kind of sexuality is meant by all this?

Why do we commonly use the expression "to make love" to describe mating where there is apparently no love? Because human beings know intuitively that sexual energy and love have the same fine level of energy. Sex is a surge, an encounter, a welcoming, a giving to the other. . . even if this level of quality is not always reached, far from it.

The energy proper to the sex center is the same as that which animates the higher emotional center, the heart. Once the heart has been unburdened of emotion, it always says "yes" to reality. Sometimes the body says "yes"; sometimes the body says "no." Swallow a mouthful of kerosene and you will spit it out immediately. The head can also say "no": no, the price is too high for my budget, I won't order that. But a purified heart knows no opposite; it knows only love. It has no negative half, contrary to the corrupt way the heart usually functions, generating ordinary emotions associated with all the painful and conflictual thoughts we know only too well.

Now the sexual function itself has no negative half either. It sees reality as either neutral and indifferent (this radiator has no effect whatsoever on your sex center) or as positive, enjoyable and agreeable. All this may sound theoretical for the moment; you may even feel that it does not correspond to your own personal experience. Only attentive observation will prove to you that the sex center in itself, just like the purified heart of a sage, knows no duality.

A perfectly unified heart sees the will of God at work everywhere. It says "yes" to everything, even if it must later act in response to a situation. What word, above all others, expresses the higher emotional center? "Yes" – like Mary's "Yes" to the Angel of Annunciation. And what word best expresses the sex center? "Yes!" I remember a private recording, which was outstanding both theatrically and erotically, in which a great actress expressed all the different stages of sexual union, from its prelude up until its final outcome, simply by varying the word "Yes" – a "yes" as voluptuous as it was metaphysical.

"Yes" is all that both the higher emotional center and the sex center know. In contrast, our ordinary functions all have a negative part. The intellectual center has two ways to say "no." One is right: "Do you want some jam?," "No, thank you. I am a diabetic and cannot eat sugar." But the intellectual center has developed the habit of saying "no" by imitation for all sorts of outer causes. And these causes have made up the personal world within which we are prisoners. We have been taught to refuse one aspect or another of reality, although there was actually no valid reason for this "no." The emotional center is encumbered with denial and we try to pacify and neutralize this denial through therapy or *lyings*. (*Lyings* is the name Swami Prajnanpad gave to a technique that he developed in order to purify the unconscious. It consists in plunging into one's unconscious, to consciously live out unconscious trauma.) As for the instinctive-moving center, it manifests its denial through contractions, inhibitions and closing up. In this manner, it says "no" to sensations that it feels are distressing because they are associated with former trauma.

Given that both higher feeling and the sex center consume the same fine energy, how is it that sexuality is generally experienced in such a negative way? Sex has been known to cause disaster in life. Just what is it that happens? Like wires that touch each other – a situation to be avoided in electricity – connections are set up between the sex center and the negative half of the other centers. All esoteric teachings (although they may not give explanations as methodical as Gurdjieff's) could be shown to confirm these facts.

Is it possible to imagine a radiant and fulfilling sex act in which one says no . . . no . . . no? If you look closely, you will see that it is not. If this does occur, it is because the sex center has entered into contact with the negative half of the intellectual center, the emotional center or the instinctive-moving center. Here is what happens:

when a given person's sex center is stimulated, it awakens a distressing emotion linked to a memory hidden away in the negative half of one of the ordinary centers with which, in the past, sex set up a connection that should not have existed. And a "no" arises. For example, one woman may let herself be caressed but might find the idea of letting a man kiss her sex unbearable, whereas another woman might see this as proof of the man's love, a sign of tenderness or a much-appreciated form of sensuality. Most often, the other centers' negative reactions are rooted in the unconscious. This is why it is necessary to make the unknown part of one's *psychism* conscious.

If you think about this characteristic of the sex center, you will realize how often sexuality can be perturbed. In actual fact, it is only in human beings that the sex act itself causes real problems. Sex is purely enjoyable for animals in nature. We have not created as many problems for seeing or hearing! The sex center becomes contaminated by energy which is not its own. If the emotional center harbors a fear of being betrayed, then the sex center – entering into contact with the ordinary emotional center – becomes afraid: "No – if I enjoy the sensations I feel, things will go wrong." Although this mechanism is absolutely absurd, it is quite common. Similarly, the sex center cannot function normally if it enters into contact with the negative part of the intellectual center and if this latter has taboos: "This is not done, it is immoral, it is giving in to man's weakness; a true saint does not have a sex life; it is shameful to make love with a woman without being in love with her . . ." the whole range of guilt and value judgements that we know only too well. If the negative part of the intellectual center interferes, sex becomes neurotic.

But it must be understood that *sex in itself* – as offered by nature to all human beings – always remains unspoiled. In itself, it is never sadistic or masochistic, although these perversions do exist. By following a spiritual path of purification and conviction to create counterorders that will be stronger than your inhibitions, you can become completely reconciled with your sexuality. This you must do, in spite of your past . . . your upbringing . . . your disappointments . . . your disastrous honeymoon night . . . your shame at having slept with rich men whom you found ugly and did not love . . . or at having made love to girls you looked down on, knowing that you would drop them the next day after promising them the night before that it would be forever . . . This you must do despite all your judgements, including what priests may have told you about masturbation.

Just as a movie screen is never affected by the film being projected, just as *anandamayakosha* is already present in you, and just as you are destined to love with a love which has no opposite – in the same way, sexual energy itself is never contaminated. Your sexuality remains perfect. I am saying this to each one of you, in particular to those who are suffering and whose problems of impotence, frigidity and total disinterest in sex are known to me. You have been cut off from your spontaneity because of unfortunate connections established with your other functions, which have themselves been considerably disturbed. If you think you have sexual problems, you are mistaken – you have psychological problems. Take heart, be reassured – not one of you has a damaged sex center. What is damaged is your mind and your emotions and it is these two that can create neurosis. You think that you have bad memories associated with sex because a family member abused you when you were a child. God knows how often Denise Desjardins (even more than I) saw proof of how many little girls or boys had been sexually perturbed by adults! It happens more often than one imagines but nothing is more censored. Yet the fact is that your sex center is never damaged; only your thoughts, heart and body can be wounded.

Sexual energy always remains fundamental energy – unscathed by trauma – before it branches out into intellectual energy, emotional energy and physical energy. There is work to be done to decondition the disturbances of the emotional center, the harmful *samskara*s engraved in the body ("I cannot stand being touched...") and the madness of the mind with its false laws which we have unconsciously decreed, and through which we live in the prison of our world instead of living in the world. But the sex center, that intact source of vitality, persistently seeks to function, just as trees blossom every spring. And it asks to be used – either through spiritual techniques which lead to fulfillment or through the mutual attraction of a man's body and a woman's body (homosexuality aside, for the time being).

The tragedy in the lives of many is that there is a contradiction between their active sex drive (which is normal) and the denial of their sexuality by the negative part of their other centers. Sexuality can help you come back to the truth of nature if you use it as a starting point, if you consider that it is unspoiled and that it can come to your aid. Insofar as you have a sex life, you can give it a chance to make you creative – provided you do not turn it into a neurotic and degraded act.

How can you free yourself from the past? What can save you is the fact that your sex center itself is never affected. And your sex center is your fundamental life force; it is what drives you toward others; it is the foundation of love which can go on to communicate directly from heart to heart and from soul to soul. Of course you may fall in love – you may become infatuated and entranced and claim to love someone – but there is no possible way you can love (in the spiritual sense of the word), unless you are fully reconciled with your sexuality. If a monk in a monastery completely accepts his sexual energy, that very energy can be transmuted and lead him to love. But those who enter a monastery either condemning sexuality or through fear of it, can pray as much as they want all day long, but they will not attain to love; they will just grow old, sad and embittered while their spiritual life turns to failure.

Sexual energy itself, unpolluted by the negative part of the other centers, is the most sacred energy of all. This is why there are so many allusions to sexuality in mysticism. Although you have every right to use this fine energy to lead a normal sex life, you must not forget its sacred nature. Do not waste it. If you have the audacity to fully respect it, sexuality will become a sacred activity for you, leading you to self-fulfillment, love, communion and non-duality. But too often, sexual energy can neither simply remain latent nor be harmoniously used in a happy union – either because your inhibitions prevent you from meeting someone or because the relationship is not good, even if the man loves the woman or the woman loves the man. So many women have told me that although they love their husbands, they cannot bear to have sexual intercourse – or only occasionally, when they feel a certain emotional balance. What must be understood is that it is the other functions that are affected and draw back; sexuality itself has nothing to do with these fears and sufferings.

$$\smile \cdot \cdot \smile$$

There are only three right ways to experience sexual energy. One of these is temporary, applying to particular circumstances in which it is impossible to have a couple relationship – but where there is actually no temptation to have sex. For example, a man may be detained in a prisoner of war camp, with only officers or soldiers, and find that his sexuality fades into the background because of the complete absence of women. My own father, a psychologist, spent a year as a prisoner in an officers' camp in 1940, before being freed because he had been wounded during the 1914-18 war. He once told me that the young officers never spoke of women; they talked mainly about food! All other than serious conversations consisted in describing the menu of their nephew's first communion feast or what they had to eat at their cousin's wedding. "Grub" was the main preoccupation because they were very badly fed. But the absence of women did not seem to cause them any great problem. Similarly, when I lived for several months at a stretch with Sonam Kazi in Bhutan or in Sikkim, meeting only Tibetan nuns with shaven heads who did not wash every day, my sexuality was temporarily dormant. In such instances, there is no harmful interference from one's other centers and periods of momentary abstinence like these are absolutely normal.

The second right way to use sexual energy is continence. As stated by Danielou (the Indian scholar, not the cardinal), "Continence is a technique, not a virtue." This is an interesting distinction. It is not particularly virtuous or admirable to lead a spiritual life which excludes sex. Even if it is inspired by love of God, continence is simply a method to obtain certain specific results. What will become of the unused energy? Thanks to the very quality of the sex center, this energy can be put into meditation. With a little spirit and determination, you can experience this yourself. If you feel a very strong sexual urge which cannot be satisfied (except by masturbation), and if you accept both the intensity of your desire and the impossibility of satisfying it (even if this demands a lot of you for twenty or thirty minutes), the quantity of the sexual energy will intensify to the extent that it will actually transmute in quality. At this point, full acceptance of the force of your desire brings about a change in levels. I can tell you for a fact that some who have heard this have tried it and succeeded. One woman had her first great meditation experience one day when she felt a particularly strong sexual urge during a retreat here. At the time, there was no man in her life. She concentrated on her desire, being completely "one with" it and without becoming afraid, and the change in quality came about. After this very rich experience, she was at peace for several consecutive days while continuing to live in the vibration of that marvelous moment which had allowed her to connect directly with what India calls *anandamayakosha*: a state of pure love and bliss.

And finally, the third way to use sexual energy is of course sexual union itself: "Be completely normal before trying to be supranormal." Like transmutation, normal and true sexual fulfillment can play a foremost role on the Way. I will come back to this point later.

So there are three possibilities from the spiritual point of view. The first (which should not be dramatized) consists in having no sex life for a certain period of time; the second is transmutation; the third is a normal sex life. Apart from these, there is something which psychologists call sublimation but which is not necessarily liberating. It is said that Beethoven composed his symphonies because he had no sex life and his libido went entirely into his work of art. We are fortunate to be able to appreciate the talent, greatness and power of the message he conveyed but this does not prove that he attained wisdom and liberation. Yet this is a socially acceptable manner, and a more or less individually acceptable one, to exploit one's sexual energy, apart from having a normal sex life or from transmuting the energy.

But what becomes of sexual energy if it is not channeled in any of these right ways? It is consumed by the other centers. This point must be absolutely clear so that you can better understand yourself. An electrical appliance cannot work on gas or fuel oil and a gas appliance will not work on electricity. But in the complexity of the human organism, such a misfortune is possible. Thought is fueled by sexual energy, although that is not the energy suited to it since thought normally uses energy which is less subtle and less intense. The ordinary emotional center, which includes all the gross emotions, works on energy that is not its own either. And so does the moving center. All of this constitutes an enormous waste.

Three characteristics permit us to detect these interferences. But before we come to them, there is something that must be clarified. At times we voluntarily take advantage of these interferences – which are harmful from a spiritual point of view – in order to obtain certain results. There is truth to the slogan: "Make love, not war." It has long been common knowledge that people would be much less belligerent if they made love well. If fighters are needed, those who are not at ease sexually will best fulfill the role. In the "struggle for life," it can be an advantage to be a sexual neurotic; one can become a "battler." This can end up creating confusion unless you examine the situation more closely.

Now we come to the three characteristics which indicate the defective functioning of our centers due to a deviation of sexual energy. First, unnecessary or unjustified intensity; secondly, a pointlessness in one's accomplishments or actions; and thirdly, a readiness to fight. Let me point out that these apply just as much to women as to men, in spite of the differences between male and female natures.

Deviated sexual energy has an aggressive aspect; consequently it is used to fight, attack or criticize. This readiness to fight is aggravated by the two other characteristics: intensity and pointlessness. If the emotional center functions on sexual energy, religion becomes a condemnation of heretics, with an exaggerated emphasis on the fate of sinners who are going to burn in hell. In other areas, there are those who become inflamed for a cause, writing satirical tracts and raging furiously in front of audiences. This deviation reveals itself through emotional fanaticism, a state of excitement and over-intensity: "That's horrible! It's appalling! It's intolerable!" Excess, fighting, and in the end, pointlessness.

If your sexual energy gets diverted to your moving center, simply vacuuming or cleaning a bathtub can turn into an all-out wrestling match with the vacuum cleaner or the bathtub. I have also often observed that there is a pointlessness that characterizes actions fed by energy which comes from other centers. For example, you might see someone holding a forty-five minute "conversation" with a person who cannot listen and cannot even hear what is being said that day, because this latter is too preoccupied with his or her own problems. The speaker is talking for nothing, without even realizing it. Such an action is like planting coins and watering them every day, hoping they will grow. Another example that relates to the moving center is this: some use their sexual energy to break records. And why not? That can be interesting, depending on one's frame of mind. But a sportsman who leads a truly fulfilling sex life does not have the same approach to sports as a sportsman whose sexual energy feeds his moving center.

These diversions of sexual energy must not be confused with transmutation which nurtures *anandamayakosha* in mystics. Neither should such diversions be confused with the contact established, during an especially harmonious sex act, between a supramental level of consciousness and orgasm itself.

All neuroses are said to be of sexual origin. To fully understand this statement, one must realize that neuroses result partly from the fact that the ordinary centers function not with their own energy, provided by nature, but rather with sexual energy, as described earlier.

And the sex center – which normally is not dual – completes the disaster. It becomes the field of expression for the other functions with their duality and their contradictions, making it possible to lead only a restricted sex life, composed of localized sensations which are both disappointing and frustrating. It is no longer the total human being who partakes in the sex act and so this act does not let one transcend and surpass oneself. I do not deny that the resulting physiological sensations can be a precious release. I will put things bluntly. Many people have confided in me as they would in a priest or a psychologist. I know certain women who have been without a man for several years and who use an artificial penis when they feel overpowered by their desire; it brings them momentary well-being. I do not condemn them at all. Apparently, I have no morals apart from seeing you truly happy once and for all, able to forget yourselves and to think of others. Someone who is happy can put another's interest before his own; someone who is frustrated and unhappy is condemned to selfishness. I wish that you may all discover the vast, the noble and even the divine – and realism without falsehood on the Way.

Although I make no judgement, the fact remains that ordinary eroticism does not help you understand why the Upanishads and metaphysics in general so often refer to union of the flesh to describe the highest mystic accomplishments. "... Like a man and woman in tender embrace, the man no longer knowing if he is a man or a woman, and the woman no longer knowing if she is a woman or a man . . ." Sacred scriptures do not hesitate to make a comparison with the sex act to describe marvelous experiences of fusion, self-surpassing and transcendence.

For my part, during the period when my sex life was normal but nothing more, I could not manage to believe that sex could be a mystic act. I was attracted by women and found that stimulating; I knew how to please and sometimes reproached myself for making one woman suffer because I wanted to court another. But in the end, it was all rather disappointing. Was it really so divine? Even in a so-called love relationship, I again ended up disappointed because the negative part of my other functions had not been sufficiently purified. What remained of the sex act once the act itself was finished?

On the other hand, if you have experienced a beyond-the-mind state during sexual intercourse, the most precious part remains after it is over. The feeling of sadness one generally feels after sex is not mentioned in sexuality as it is described in Indian teachings – and they are very explicit on the subject. The gradual increase and climax normally felt (especially for the man, or for the woman in clitoral sex), on the contrary opens out onto another plane, even if this happens only rarely. I am not saying that this never happens, but confidences entrusted to those who take an interest in such questions plus serious publications on the matter as well as my own experience of listening to others show that it is not frequent. Nevertheless, certain women who have no interest whatsoever in metaphysics but whose neurosis is not expressed in the sex act, give lyrical descriptions of their orgasms – descriptions which resemble mystical accounts and make other women, who have never had such experiences, dream. Generally speaking, women are more often sexually inhibited than men. Yet, in return, men are much less capable of exalted and refined sexuality and there are more unprepared women than there are unprepared men who reach beyond-the-mind states during the sexual act.

Let us have a look at the case of one sexually-inhibited woman. Any sexual stimulation – or almost any, except under conditions when she is exceptionally relaxed and confident – awakens in her the normal desire, but at the same time it also awakens a connection with the negative part of one (or two, or the three) of her ordinary centers. This woman may well be quite charming with her partner, provided she feels no sexual desire for a few days. But as soon as her own desire arises, negative reactions are immediately stimulated and she begins to find her partner unbearable, without understanding what is happening inside her. Her mind takes hold of this momentary repulsion, makes a great deal of fuss over it, keeps turning over the past and projecting onto the future, only to make the whole situation worse. Not only is it impossible for the woman in question to have a full and harmonious sex life but furthermore, the deviated energy makes her emotional and mental disturbances worse. Both she and her companion will therefore need to use much skill in order to be at ease together once more.

Our love life remains unsatisfactory because of these bad connections. Sexual energy is neither used by the sex center nor transmuted and it wrongly feeds our other functions. And this use of the sexual center's energy by our ordinary centers creates a tension, an excess, a readiness to fight and a pointlessness which nurture the obstacles to normal satisfaction. This entire interaction gives the impression of a vicious circle from which it is impossible to escape.

From a technical point of view, your work will therefore be to stop appeals to the sex center from activating negative reactions in the other centers. These reactions actually have no relationship with the sex center. It is right and natural to feel sexual desire arise in you; after that you can see, in relation to the various parameters of your life, if you will follow through with your desire or not. Do not ruin your future by letting yourself be overwhelmed and swept away by a rising desire, making you do things which will have serious consequences. And do not deny your sexual demands either.

But it is a sorry thing for your sexual fulfillment if an appeal to your sex center connects you to negative reactions rooted in your unconscious.

So the question becomes quite specific. How is it possible to avoid interference from the negative half of the moving center, the intellectual center or the emotional center – or from all three at the same time? Any work you do on the negative half of these centers will have a beneficial effect on your sex life. And in general, the "way" as a whole will help purify these centers. Each time you try to change denial into acceptance or tenseness into relaxation, each time you challenge one of the prejudices or the alleged laws which make up your subjective world – even if it has apparently no direct relation with your love life – you are contributing to your future sexual fulfillment. I am not saying that your love life will be miraculously transformed if your glasses broke when they fell and you accepted that fact without emotion. But if you definitively get into the habit of saying "yes" to what is, that "yes" will end up per-meating your life and lessening the negative force of your other centers.

Unfortunately, once denial becomes established, it does not dis-appear so quickly. This is why it is necessary to undertake a true *sadhana* (spiritual practice), which may eventually include work on your unconscious. But at least if you realize how strong your reactions are, plus the fact that they are abnormal, you will know how to orient your efforts and you will know just what you can expect from *lyings*. Of course *lyings* will indirectly have a beneficial effect on your sexuality, even if you do not directly work on that area, because they teach you to let go of your old fears. But for *lyings* to be effective for you, they must be based on a deep-rooted acceptance. The goal is certainly not to stay on the level of "Bastard, bastard! Dad, you are a bastard!" Abreactions like this are only a preparation. *Lyings* which are really liberating are ones which result in a "yes" to everything: "'Yes' to suffering, 'yes' to fear, 'yes' to despair, 'yes' to Mom's death when I was four years old, 'yes' to Dad's terrifying anger when I was six. . ."

A therapist gave me two photographs of a woman I do not know. One, taken during a *lying* session, showed her face twisted in suffering; the other, taken just after the session, revealed a face so luminous and internalized that one wondered if the woman had just had a fantastic orgasm or if she was in *samadhi*. I had noticed this myself after certain intense *lyings* I had accompanied. It can only happen if there has been an unconditional "yes" to all that had theoretically been a cause of suffering for the person re-experiencing old and forgotten trauma.

Each of you can ask himself or herself this: in what way does the negative half of one of my centers still manage to interfere? And there, I assure you that a new understanding of the nobleness of sexuality can be a help. In the pure state of love, peace, bliss and reconciliation which is beyond ordinary emotions, there exists a quality of "yes" that can also be found in a happy and spontaneous sex act with no mental reservations, with all the eroticism that such a "yes" may contain. A totally different connection can thus be established between sex and the heart itself. It is for this reason that there can be a marvelous feeling after certain really fulfilling sex acts, both on the sex level and on the heart level, even for people who take no interest whatsoever in a spiritual path.

Sex and the heart have a similar non-duality which allows them to fuse if the sex center functions with its own energy. This explains the use of sex in certain Tantric practices where the goal is to surpass the habitual level of consciousness. In this specific context, sexual relations between partners can take place outside a lasting marital relationship. Mankind, particularly in India, has tried everything. In certain Tantric practices – ones which are definitely not forms of debauchery but which remain secret and are not exported to the West – the sexual act must take place between a man who does not know the woman at all and a woman who does not know the man at all, so that it will be the man in him, who meets the woman in her, and vice versa, without causing reactions in the other centers.

Remember that the sex drive is natural. As Swamiji said: "*It is but normal and natural.*" One of Jean Cocteau's poems which moved me when I was young starts like this: "If you love, poor child, do not fear; it is the universal law." No matter how neurotic you are, your sexual energy does not disappear. There are differences of course; it can be more or less strong in different human beings. As a rule, the stronger your sexual drive, the more qualified you are for yoga or mysticism. This is the reason why eunuchs were not allowed to become priests or monks. But in fact, most human beings have a strong sex center, even if it is repressed, because the sex center has the distinctive characteristic of working with very fine energy. The sex act or a sex life could therefore normally constitute a very rich "*food of impressions.*"

⁓

Whatever may be your difficulties in the sexual domain, look fearlessly at the truth. To regain this childlike spontaneity to which you aspire, you must neutralize the negative connections which have already become established. Start with the grossest ones – those which weigh on you although they are not directly rooted in your unconscious. In particular, this involves all the value judgements which condemn or slight sexuality: it is wrong, it is vulgar, it is a sin. As a support to help you counterbalance these preconceived ideas, take in new concepts: it is good, God is with me, I am not afraid to feel. As many theologians realize, the great mistake of historical Christianity was to have hardened the words of St. Paul – which often corresponded to specific circumstances – and to have just barely tolerated sex as a necessary concession for bringing children into the world.

Try using opposite convictions to help make your false ideas disappear, even if these latter have not been sapped at the foundations through *lyings*. And see what happens . . . see what still comes up physically, emotionally or mentally in you to suggest: "No, no, you must not feel things with all your being." You can also orient your *lyings* directly onto a subject, if you know what you want to recall. "Just what does 'I must not' mean? That's not true! My parents were what they were, the Catholic education I received corresponded to the ideas of my social background, but what does ancient wisdom say?" And after all, what did Christ really say? You will become like a little child again if you get rid of what stops you from being natural. An "underground order," to use Denise Desjardins' eloquent expression, will warn you: "No!" How can you rediscover your childlike spontaneity, not in little diversions but in an adult game which can become grandiose? Even though it is rare, you can aspire to divine sexuality where childlike simplicity has a role to play.

Each time you dare to be as happy as a child, even aside from any sexual connotation, you are favoring this blossoming which you have so rightly sensed. Dare to be a child! Not childish, childlike. Dare. I had to meet Swamiji to dare to order an ice cream with whipped cream, hot chocolate and a cherry instead of soberly ordering "two scoops of vanilla" in a café. Never would I have been able to do it, if I had not met that Hindu Swami. . . "It's not right to spend money like that on desserts!" What a blessing it is each time you have the audacity to become childlike once again! But you must use your intelligence: "No! It is not wrong. Christ himself says it is right! Why should I try to out-Herod Herod, or to out-Christ Christ?" Intelligence can help you if you had a religious upbringing, as I did.

If you watch a child playing, you will be amazed to see how much he lives in the present! He does not anticipate what is going to happen two minutes later. Naturally, it may sound strange to talk of technique or effort for what should be spontaneous. Still, we can become more simple by trying to experience things which have a sexual connotation in a second-to-second way. Each gesture can be made for itself and not in relation to the next step. Otherwise the gesture is not really experienced in purity and innocence. If a woman caresses a man's knee and he thinks: "When is she going

to caress my sex?," what a mistake! By living in expectation, by seeing each gesture only as a preparation, you miss the perfection of
the moment. Projecting yourself into a future which is one minute,
ten seconds, or even two seconds from now, is enough to lose the
preciousness of the moment itself.

There is one more important point. Sexuality between a man
and a woman – even between Christian spouses who have decided
to sanctify their marriage by the Church sacrament or have put an
icon in their bedroom – should be completely free. There should
be no restriction whatsoever between spouses. Even at the beginning of this century, certain attempts made by the clergy to deter-
mine what was permissible or not bordered on the absurd.
Ecclesiastics who had never touched a woman decreed among
themselves whether it was permitted to caress a woman's vagina
with an entire finger or with only part of the finger. When there is
love. . . during the love act. . . everything should be possible.
Children play because they dare to take every liberty: "ZZOOOOM-
MMMM. . . I'm an airplane" they say, spreading their arms for the
wings. They do not stop to ask if it is permissible or not.

A monogamous marriage, where the partners are faithful to
each other, has a sacred character in India also. God knows how
chaste and modest the traditional Hindu woman is; she would feel
dishonored if she physically aroused any man other than her
husband. Yet in this context of modesty and refinement, Swamiji
said (and of course it is valid for both sexes): *"For her husband,
a wife is everything that all women can be for a man. If he is sick, she
becomes a nurse; if he has work and she helps him, she is an associate;
if he is tired or sad, she plays the role of mother; if he explains to her
certain things that she does not know, she becomes a daughter,"* and
Swamiji added: *"and a mistress."* But to another among us he said
"a courtesan" and to yet another *"a prostitute."* And the husband, of
course, should also play all these roles for his wife. The India
that I knew was not male chauvinist. In her role as a mother,

a woman is actually considered divine. And God, in India, is just as much a Mother as he is a Father.

You can attain this childlike simplicity only if you can convince yourself to surpass all the images and restrictions which arouse inner denial. In the communion of bodies and hearts, there should be no rule except spontaneity and a great welcome for the spontaneity of the other. This surpassing of what could arouse denial comes from a decision that any ever-so-slightly advanced disciple can make. "Oh no! . . . Oh yes!" Even "No, you're hurting me!" can blossom into "Yes! Yes! Yes!" The "hurt" in question changes in an instant – unless the husband is truly awkward and brutal, be it inadvertently. The only way to rediscover your own transparency is by completely accepting that of the other. Spontaneity is childlike freedom, the letting-go of the mind, broadened awareness . . . but it is not being swept away. If you are aware and inventive, you will be inspired, like a child playing. But each partner must feel that there are no restrictions. Imagine a woman who suddenly feels like singing in the middle of the sex act. "What's come over her ?" Ah, but not at all! The man might even dare to join in and together they may improvise the melody of a blessed moment. "What? That's not in my manual. It says that you should know the erogenous zones and that they change according to the different astrological signs, but it doesn't say anywhere that you have to sing." No – but then spontaneity has nothing to do with sex manuals.

It is a decision you must take. The first step is the hardest: "I'll dare . . . I dared and it went well." Nothing is needed except the agreement and complicity of the two partners. You will see how much richer this freedom is, compared to searching for erotic innovations. Some couples hesitate over whether it is more exciting if the woman is dressed in black lace or only half-dressed, whether or not to put mirrors on the ceiling or what is the best type of lighting. These are mediocre by-products of spontaneity. In such cases the sex center, instead of using its own fine energy, uses the much

91

less refined energy of thought, emotion or even of the moving center. Thought comes in, with its characteristic dualism and slowness, and invents so-called refinements. Just what is the intellectual center doing there, with images and memories which rob you of the present moment? "It's going to be so exciting!" Not at all! It is not a mistake in itself to take certain details into account – like the fact that if the man likes a certain type of nightgown, it may have a greater affect on him – but this confines sexuality to a grosser level, connecting it with ordinary perceptions and conceptions which are never by any means transcendental. Just what is transcendental? The higher emotional center in Gurdjieff's language, *anandamayakosha* to use the Sanskrit term, and the sex center when it is not linked to the disturbances of the other functions. The sex center does not need these frills which actually represent demands from the other centers. Do not condemn them, experiment a little, take them into account, but do so in order to transcend them because they cut you off from spontaneity and from total freedom from the past.

On the other hand, if an urge arises which, so to speak, is not on the program, dare to accept and experience it. Let there be no censorship in sexuality, none other than mutual love, that is, taking the other into account. Let me repeat that in sex, like in rituals, all the senses are involved.

Remember that there are three apparently very different activities which simultaneously affect the five senses: sexual union, which has a sacred dimension, the liturgy and cooking, which is also sacred for Hindus. If you listen to a record, it only appeals to your ears; if you inhale a Guerlain perfume (the publicity is free) it appeals only to your sense of smell; if you taste a wine, it appeals to sight, smell and taste but not touch (a wine taster does not dip his fingers into a great vintage to feel its liquidness) and wine produces no sound.

In rituals, *pujas* and religious worship, the five senses participate equally. Incense is for the nose; the decor, vestments, accessories and ceremony are for the eyes; there is chanting and music for the ears. Touch is also involved: Tibetans turn prayer wheels, Orthodox Catholics caress or kiss the church icons one after the other, Moslems touch their hand to the tombstones of the different saints. And there is always the partaking of a sacrament – a holy bread, a consecrated substance or a liquid. The five senses are involved at the same time . . . thus the four elements . . . and so the whole of creation.

Orientals have been audacious enough to say that the five senses participate in the sex act (*maithuna* in Sanskrit), and they have even given very realistic details. There is the sense of taste with the intake of the other's saliva; there is smell with the erotic stimulant of the odor of male or female secretions; there is hearing in the sounds and words that are voiced, touch through caresses and physical contact and sight since the other is looked at. Sex therefore offers us a very important opportunity to change to a sensual and sensory level – not just a sexual one – and so to leave behind the mind which maintains us within contradiction, conflict and time. The sex act has been compared to meditation because it enables us to eliminate thought and to be in communion through the five senses here and now. This is an idea which often shocks people and arouses reactions: "What do you mean? I don't want to see when I'm making love; you're supposed to do it in the dark!" Why should one make love in the dark? Why are you afraid to look and to contemplate? Sight is part of sex, and so is smell. Why refuse a specific smell that accompanies the rise of desire and that can come from a man's sex even if he takes a bath every day? An uninhibited woman finds this natural smell attractive. Is it so very repulsive to kiss a woman's sex and to take female secretions into one's mouth?

I realize that in speaking realistically, I am putting many of you ill-at-ease. Yet we are dealing here with truths which have been recognized traditionally. Sexuality will be spontaneous only if your mind imposes no bans and above all, if it does not decide in advance how things should come about. Nothing is forbidden. It is false to think in that matter. You have been lied to, in good faith. What is important is fulfillment; what is important is "yes," a word of love and non-duality. Do not hesitate to use the very thing which, from one viewpoint, has done you so much wrong: the predominance of the intellect over what is sensory and sensual. Do not hesitate to use intellectual understanding to correct the mind. Intellectual certainty, born from a vision which is free from the coloring of past circumstances, can convince even the heart and the body.

5

THE EVER-PURE SPRING

ALL spiritual teachings are unanimous on certain points. Living in the present, the here and now, which implies being free from the past is one of these points. You are probably familiar with this concept; it is certainly not specific to Swami Prajnanpad alone. The weight of the past hinders us from being at ease, natural and whole. But although most teachings presented in metaphysical form do not specify it, the fact of the matter is that the past means our own past and that to be free from the past is to be free from one's own personal past. Maybe this is clear for you. Although I may sound naive, I must admit that during all those years before I met Swami Prajnanpad I myself had quite simply not realized what this meant. I was immersed in teachings that emphasized freedom and evoked the need to live in a present uncolored by the past. And if you are free of the past, you are free of the future. But I had not understood that the past meant my own past. (It could eventually include traces of past lives – that cannot be denied – but it is primarily the past of this present life.) What I discovered with Swamiji was how to enter into this very concrete truth – into what had happened to me, Arnaud, and what I had experienced in my own past – in spite of that little reluctance I felt at leaving behind spirituality or pure metaphysics in order to enter into what I saw as psychology or psychoanalysis.

The past this deals with means the person we used to be. It does not mean events, situations and trauma, it refers to a human being . . . a little child who became an adolescent and who went on to become a young man or a young woman discovering sexual life and professional life. That human being of bygone days lives on in you, complete with the sufferings, joys, disappointments and hardships he or she experienced. But let me repeat that it is not events that I want to emphasize, it is the happy or sad child you once were. You continue to be that very real human being. He or she lives on in you with his or her grief, fear and limitations. Yet these no longer have any reason to exist today – first of all, because you are an adult, and furthermore, because you have the help of teachings based on personal transformation.

My interactions with you have little by little led me to rediscover in a different light what I myself experienced with Swamiji: an affirmative inner force, of which you are not conscious, stands in the way of your own metamorphosis. We are all convinced that we want to stop being childish. Personally I wanted to stop being a little boy forever in search of his mother, with my life built on one basic theme: I was divinely happy until the age of two and I lost everything when my little brother was born; I searched desperately for happiness because I knew it existed, but even though I was convinced that I would find it, I also knew that I would lose it because I knew that happiness was destined to be lost. I no longer wanted to be imprisoned by those old mechanisms; I wanted to become an adult. I had told Swamiji that I was sure of that at least, even if it seemed to bring my metaphysical pretensions down a notch. But in you – just as in me – the desire to stop being that child of the past coincides with a very powerful force which refuses the change; it refuses – to say the word – to abandon that little being who still lives on inside us.

What terrorizes us, not as free beings who assume responsibility for our own lives but as dependent and still childish beings, is the fear of being abandoned. "My mother abandoned me to take care of a horrible little newborn baby." We have no intention of committing a crime against ourselves in our own turn: "Never! What you are asking of me, Arnaud, never! I was the only one who did not abandon that little child and then that adolescent. And to free myself from the past, you are asking me today to desert that little child I carry inside!"

Unless you see this very clearly, you will not understand what is keeping you from letting go and finally becoming an adult. A very strong voice in you shouts: "I will continue to protect this sad little child, this bruised and disappointed teenager that I carry within me". . . as if there were two: both the child of yesterday and the adult of today. The image of a caterpillar dying to become a butterfly does not terrify you because you feel that flying is much better than crawling on the ground. But you do not really feel that the childish being in you is going to die so that you can become adult. If only the transformation were felt in this way: "I want to stop being dependent, I want to stop being vulnerable, I want to become truly mature and to be in full possession of myself," then the way would be much quicker and you would not face such inner resistance.

Perhaps you remember this story I have often told. I happened to be at Swamiji's ashram on my forty-second birthday and a man named Nandakishore asked me, "What would you like for a birthday present?" It reminded me that I had one day asked the same question of Sumongal, an Indian who was at the ashram on his fortieth birthday. He had answered: "What I would like for my fortieth birthday is to be really forty years old." I had been so struck by his answer that I felt the need to tell it to Swamiji at the beginning of my daily talk with him on my own birthday. And I suddenly felt overwhelmed and burst out sobbing: it was unbearable. Unbearable that at forty-two years of age I was so far from being forty-two. "Where's Mommy, where's Mommy?. . ." Having said this, I must point out that this happened at a time in my life when I was asserting myself with ease; I would not want to give you a ridiculous image of the television producer I was then who actually appeared to be becoming more adult. Yet there, across from Swamiji, I suddenly understood that for my forty-second birthday what I really wanted was simply to be two years old. If I were really forty-two on my forty-second birthday, then that was the end of that endearing little child with whom I had lived through all the ages of my life, the child with whom I had gone to school, the child who was sometimes happy, sometimes sad, full of dreams at fourteen, and crying at twenty because he'd been rejected by a girl . . . . And that is what we cannot bear. Yet it is the truth. You cannot be fully forty-two, and at the same time tenderly keep that little child inside, consoling him yourself, as if it were up to you to pamper and protect him.

Try to remember how – even at a young age and without realizing it – you had to comfort yourself, you had to become a companion for yourself when you were alone, curling up in your own arms and withdrawing into yourself. When you were only small, you had to take care of yourself because Mom and Dad had gone to the movies, leaving you all alone at home . . . "Mom and Dad don't care about me". . . . As far as the emotion of being abandoned is concerned (I'll be left all alone, I'll be betrayed), becoming an adult means that you yourself are going to abandon and betray that little child whom you have carried within yourself to this very day. There is thus a very powerful force which refuses such a metamorphosis. Leaving the past behind, turning the page and being our real age means no longer being six, no longer being twelve and no longer being twenty. Try to feel what I am saying. It is as if you were being asked to commit the greatest of all crimes: to abandon that lonely little child . . . "Bye bye, au revoir, finished, I'm leaving you all alone." Alongside your legitimate aspiration to stop being a childish adult – with all the selfishness, dependency and inability to give that characterizes a childish adult – you have the unbearable impression that you are being asked to give the final knife thrust to the sad little boy inside, then to the idealistic and unhappy teenager and finally to the man who, later on, staggered under the blows of his career and his love life.

Your impression that you are going to betray the one you carry within you is false. You must therefore look into it very carefully.

It is the very nature of that little child to grow up and become an adult but trauma and painful wounds have hindered that growth. What you must feel is not that you are going to betray the child inside but just the opposite: the greatest act of love that I can show this little girl or this little boy is to help her, to help him, grow up and fulfill what he or she longs for. I do not want to become an adult to the detriment of that little inner child (in which case I have the impression that I am the one who is pitilessly rejecting it); it is the goal of that little child himself to become an adult; it is his or her reason for living. And the best gift I can offer the child still crying at the bottom of my heart is to tell him: "You are going to be able to open up, to blossom, you are going to fulfill your own nature." Give up your false idea that the child "dies" so that the adult can unfold, just as the caterpillar must die for the butterfly to unfold. With just cause, that seems as cruel to you as killing a bull in the arena: "For forty years I have been trying to console that child in every possible way – I have found him a woman to love him, I have given him the applause of an audience, I have given him whatever satisfactions I had the money to buy him. I have taken care of him as best I could, and now you are asking me to plunge a knife into him like a matador plunges a knife into a bull. Impossible!"

As long as this conviction remains all-powerful in your subconscious, you will resist letting yourself mature with all your might. You will refuse to turn the page on the past, as called for in all spiritual teachings, because you cannot agree to commit a crime against what is dearest to you, against a child only you have never betrayed and only you have always loved. Take the opposite viewpoint. It is not the triumph of the adult in you over the child in you; it is the triumph of the child who has the chance to blossom and catch up to you as an adult.

Every path of evolution asks you to turn the page on what is past. If you do not do so, you will never become a sage; you will become a childish old man or old woman, who withers away without ever having blossomed. You must go back to that wounded little girl or that wounded little boy, to that sensitive and emotional teenager, equally prone to flights of enthusiasm or bouts of despair: "For years you have wanted to grow up, for years you have wanted to blossom, for years the little stalk inside has wanted to become a great tree . . . I am going to give that to you." It is not the death of the caterpillar to free the butterfly, it is the triumph of the caterpillar. Out of love for the little boy or the little girl that you carry inside, you are going to lead it to its own fulfillment. "I am giving you your glory; you are going to be able to become vast, to live and to love; you are destined for that. The mind and your wounds have hindered you from growing, and now I myself am taking away what has stood in the way of your fulfillment." Do it for the child that you still carry in your heart.

Realistically, we can stop trying to do the impossible and instead concentrate on what all teachings declare necessary: freeing ourselves from the past. And if the weight of the past is lifted, there is no future either. Fears and preoccupations about the future are nothing but an extension of the past. We interpret and foresee the future in relation to the past. So if we are free of the past, not only do we no longer project it onto the present, but we no longer project it onto the future. To be free is to live entirely in the present, free from the past of twenty years ago and free from the past of two seconds ago, free from the future in five years from now and free from the future in two seconds. Never mind about freeing yourself from the future: freedom from the future comes of its own accord if the past no longer weighs on you.

Everyone has a past – be it a Tibetan, a Hindu or a Zen monk entering a monastery at the age of twenty-five. Here we are talking about a general past, which is more or less common to everyone. Even with a relatively normal and healthy mind, you have all known joys and sorrows, you have made a distinction between what you liked and what you did not like, you have divided the world into good and bad. But as well as this, you each have a specific past: one was psychologically killed by his father who one day went into a terrifying fit of anger, another was abandoned by her mother who put her into the care of a nurse, still another became an orphan at the age of five. It is this specific past which is brought to the surface in *lyings* or psychotherapy.

Yet not all disciples committed to a spiritual path do *lyings*; not all lie down to rediscover past experiences complete with their emotional impact; not all practice "primal scream" therapy or abreaction like in the beginnings of Freud's psychoanalysis. And still, without exception, all try to free themselves from the past. So do not use only *lyings* for your liberation, even though Swami Prajnanpad put this method at our disposal as part of a complete *sadhana*. Use all that is offered, all that is available to you. I am not talking about methods which are interesting in themselves but which do not concern you. For example, none of you here intend to do the Tibetan three-year retreat or live in a Zen monastery and sit in zazen for several hours a day.

Of course it does seem unusual for a spiritual path like that of Swami Prajnanpad, which claims to be rooted in the Upanishads and the Yoga-Vasistha, to suggest using a method valued by psychoanalysis or modern therapies. And the majority of those who have done *lyings* have thought them to be *the* sadhana (in the singular) to free oneself from the past. This is not so. As I have often said, you can understand all Swamiji's teachings without doing *lyings*. To start with, Swamiji himself never did any.

Secondly, it may be unfortunate for you, but it is not Swami Prajnanpad who is your guru; it is Arnaud. Having Swamiji as your guru means having Swamiji there in front of you, defying you, corncring you in your contradictions and attacking your mind without mercy, while at the same time he is full of love for your ego, infinite love. But what I realized little by little – and I have often mentioned this – is that there were others besides Swami Prajnanpad in my life: there was Ramdas and Ma Anandamayi, the Gurdjieff groups and yoga, Tibetan rinpoches and Sufi pirs. I have thus practiced many different forms of meditation and although these did not lead me to the root of my mind, they did nonetheless play a certain role. Only after sixteen years of various *sadhanas* did I meet Swami Prajnanpad. Of course without Swamiji and without *lyings*, I do not know where I would be today. But before meeting him, I had already accomplished a certain amount of work which he did not have to make me do and which I continued on my own. For example, each time I had the chance I was in the habit of coming back to right posture; I practiced relaxing physical tensions, as insisted on in the Gurdjieff groups; there was also the breathing I had practiced in yoga, even if I no longer meditated systematically every day. So it is not only all I experienced with Swamiji, but the whole of my own progression that allows me to place myself in front of you today and possibly to help you.

Meditation has been brought back here at the ashram to give you a stable basis that can be a help in freeing yourself from the past. Some have been dumbstruck by these two daily meditations, as though they had always been waiting for them. Others have had difficulty, finding the meditations unrewarding and feeling that these were not part of Swamiji's path. I have been told: "You don't mention them in your early books; you even wrote that meditation was a state which came of itself when the obstacles to it had been neutralized." As it happens, *Vasanakshaya* (the erosion of desires) and *chitta shuddhi* (the purification of the unconscious) deal with wearing away the obstacles to meditation. Whatever makes us think of something else or makes it impossible for us to keep still, is an obstacle. The meditations I suggest to you are in fact linked to my own progression, my own understanding, my own *sadhana* with Swamiji. They also result from the progressive synthesis of all I have received from the different traditions with which I have come into contact.

Do not forget that what is commonly called meditation (something we understand very little until we actually practice it) helps Zen disciples and Tibetan or Hindu yogis free themselves from the past. The common points are keeping still and the meditation posture itself. This latter seems to be more or less similar on all paths. At one time or another, all meditation techniques emphasize breathing: exhaling deeply while centering one's breath in the *hara*, *pranayama*, slowing down breathing, holding one's breath. On Mount Athos, in hesychasm (the Orthodox mystic tradition), prayer based on the repetition of God's name is accompanied by breathing. Indeed, a misunderstanding of such abdominal breathing exercises has often led to criticism of the monks of Mount Athos for "contemplating their navels."

Swamiji used to say: *"Eating is a function of life, breathing is life itself."* If you let go as you exhale and expand your chest, breathing can become infinite. This is the very movement of life: a renewal in which you die each time you exhale and are recreated each time you inhale. And we can go along with this ceaseless, natural movement because our breathing continues even if we are asleep or unconscious.

But how can exercises for breathing and keeping still help you to become free of the past – of your own personal past? Here, let me mention something that I did not discover, something that is well-known to a certain number of physical therapists. The past is engraved in our breathing; it has left its mark on our breathing. It is said that God breathed on clay to create man. Yet that very beautiful movement of breathing, of breath, has been compromised by each of us in our own way, during the course of our own lives. Let me give you another personal example of an incident that came back to me. It concerns my own mother whose face suddenly became unrecognizable for me as a two-year-old. Among the brief notes I took in English when at Swamiji's ashram, there is this sentence: "Vision of nightmare, my mother has been changed." In a *lying*, I saw the face of my mother a few hours after the birth of her second baby, who was clinging to her breast. It was atrocious for the child I then was. She gazed at me without seeing me and I no longer recognized her. It literally took my breath away. For that trauma to re-emerge, it took three *lyings* of suffocation during which I thought I was going to smother to death. Do not worry, nature takes good care of things: just when I was really going to suffocate, my breathing came back by itself. Until then, I had had a vital capacity of two and a half liters on the spirometer, which is very little and very humiliating for a young man. I was incapable of exhaling. I had a hollow chest and a sort of respiratory twitch which forced me to catch my breath every four or five minutes. Apart from that, I was quite normal – and all the more so at the age of forty, when I took real pleasure in the adventuresome life I was leading. Traveling up and down the roads of Afghanistan, the Himalayas and India, I felt I could breathe again. Those *lyings* of suffocation were definitely a great help to me but if you practice a return to full breathing in meditation, it can free you from the past much more than you imagine.

We do not voluntarily decide to breathe; our respiration is taken care of by our diaphragm and thorax muscles. These muscles receive "underground orders" from the unconscious, which stop them from functioning normally. So, like muscles that have never been used, they waste away. If you are confined to bed for a year, you will have considerable difficulty in walking once you are allowed to get up. Because the muscles of the rib cage lose their full capacity, because they stiffen and waste away, the breathing of the majority of human beings is actually seriously jeopardized. Meditation goes along the lines of a return to the truth of breathing. Even apart from a civilization like ours which is so little spiritually-oriented, every Japanese, every Tibetan and every Hindu – both in the past as well as today – has had a childhood and has undergone certain disturbances of the respiratory function (although perhaps less serious than our own) which are linked to the past.

A child's vitality is linked to his breathing. The life force and spontaneity of a child are immense. He runs, climbs up and down on an armchair ten times over, jumps, climbs back up on the armchair, jumps again – all for its own sake. Of course, a minimum amount of upbringing is necessary. Yet when you restrain a child, it has an effect on his breathing and particularly on crying or shouting which are important functions for a child. If he falls, he cries; if he cannot have something, he cries; if another little boy jostles him, he cries. So he is told: "Stop crying!" or "Stop screaming!" The only way that the child you used to be was able to stop crying or screaming was by holding his breath. A little child who is crying and sobbing profusely can only stop his tears and his sobs by swallowing his breath until it becomes nothing but a poor little sniffle. When a child starts to sob to attract attention, his parents will inevitably ask him to stop sooner or later. And so, out of fear that they will get angry or out of love for his mommy who is pleading with him to cheer up, the child holds his breath. Try to rediscover the sad child in yourself and then ask yourself to stop crying. You will see that it will take you a minute to be able to breathe properly again.

The goal in meditation is little by little to bring ease back into our breathing, to make it able to "ex-press" (to "press out") once more. Expressing does not only consist in yelling during therapy; to exhale is also to express yourself. If you hold your breath, you tend to do it when inhaling thus centering yourself in the upper chest with your belly pulled in. . . and with all the tension this includes. Letting go, so well-described by Karlfried Graf Dürckheim in the book *Hara: the Vital Center of Man*, implies going back down into your abdomen and letting the movement of breathing out regain its full amplitude. Certain practices can help you re-educate your breathing, thus completing and enriching what *lyings* may have done for you. Do not deny yourself this aid because breathing not only brings air to the physical body, it also brings *prana* to the subtle body (*sukshma sharir*) and the breath of the Holy Spirit to the causal body (*karana sharir*). It nourishes the three bodies, *anandamayakosha* included. Breathing is the most sacred of all functions. This is why mystics put such emphasis on breath.

Our breathing has been impaired by our own personal past. To be a prisoner of the past is to breathe badly; being free of the past lets you breathe normally, naturally, like a baby who has not been traumatized and is sleeping peacefully, his belly rising and falling. In his book, Dürckheim superbly describes this centering in the hara as a process that enables one to accept the shocks of life much more easily and to remain even-tempered, whether the news is good or bad. Breathing exercises help you free yourself from your own past. Your inner child is most often a bruised and wounded little being (his classmates made fun of him at school, he felt abandoned by his mother and misunderstood by his father) and he is no longer able to breathe properly. Let me put it this way: a childish adult does not know how to breathe; an adult worthy of the name breathes freely. A childish adult suffers from breathing in an obstructed and deformed way; an adult has rediscovered how to breathe freely.

⌣ · ⌣

One further point: breathing is linked to a highly important but often perturbed function – sexuality. Frederick Leboyer, who studied breath in detail, observed the similarity between a mother's breathing when she is giving birth in a reunified way (which proves to be a great experience for her) and breathing during the sex act. Most of the yoga *pranayamas,* which include both deep and shallow breaths, were found in the complete sex act, particularly in women. In any case, it can be stated that there is a tie between breathing and making love.

Although I am not a pediatrician, I have noticed what joy completely normal little boys or girls can get from touching their genitals. Some educators have come to the conclusion that it is best not to interfere and I am convinced they are right. It does of course seem strange to see a little three-year-old girl fondling herself with a beaming smile on her face. Not all mothers and fathers have given a lot of thought to this matter so it is probable that the childish sexuality of many among you was frustrated by those who brought you up – and this has taken its toll on your breathing. Most adolescents have masturbated and, if there is a real letting go, masturbation brings about a change in breathing.

Listen to me with an open heart. There is no point in always pretending that certain realities which are less highly-esteemed than meditation do not exist. We do not really let go because there is almost always a taboo that produces guilt, whether we were told so in black and white or whether we guessed it. Furthermore, many young people sleep in the same room as their brother or sister, for example, or in a boarding school dormitory, and many adolescents have masturbated while completely restricting the possible respiratory manifestations so that their brother in the nearby bed would not suspect anything. Perhaps these details make you ill-at-ease. If so, it proves that this concerns you somewhat. Your more or less repressed childish sexuality, followed by a more or less badly-experienced adolescent sexuality, have ended up making you wary of your breathing. You have learned to restrain it, just as you did in your early childhood so that you could stop crying when Mom or Dad asked you to – be it nicely or severely. So even for those who may be practicing a type of yoga which recommends abstaining from sexual relations, there is a link between the natural simplicity of our relation to sexuality and our breathing. Whether your sex life is somewhat impaired because you have not rediscovered spontaneous breathing or whether you are a totally-abstaining yogi, in both cases, meditation – in which breathing plays a dominant role – helps us become natural again.

The meditation posture, in its hieratical dignity, seems artificial at first sight; the positions our bodies take mechanically feel more natural. Yet it is in this immobile position that you will find the way back to nature and become yourself again. First be natural, then aim for the supernatural. The only way to become reconciled with your breathing is to accept the existence of your sex center, which is the center of creativity for a yogi living in chastity just as it is for a man or woman with an active sex life. And hopefully your sex life is fulfilling for each of you.

Remember: creation, creativity, procreation. Someone who is not free of his past is not creative. . . or he is neurotically creative. Every human being is meant to be creative; this is not something reserved for artists who compose symphonies or draw paintings. And as we have seen, sexual energy is needed for creativity – be it to procreate a child, to procreate the new man in oneself or to accomplish a work of art.

There is thus a relation among the psychological blocks of our past, our breathing, our ease in assuming our sexuality and our capacity to be innovative. And there is a radical difference between creativity and agitation; you can be active and do lots of things yet create nothing. For example, from a certain point of view, thought creates mental consequences in us, it generates karma; it can perturb but it does not create anything. Only from the moment when it is put into concrete form by the hand of a sculptor or an artist, does it become creative. A dancer is creative, even if there is nothing left of his dance when he finishes dancing. To create is not only to leave some concrete work behind.

You can do an enormous number of things without being creative. Even if you invented the atomic bomb, it does not mean that you are creative. The terrible thing in some careers is not to feel creative, even though you work a lot. "I've typed letters, done paperwork, telephoned. . ." or "I've been to meetings and increased my rubber sales on the Manila market, working out of Paris and via Tokyo; I'm a big businessman yet my life is nothing but repetition, day in and day out." On the other hand, if you grow four tomato plants in your garden, the budding and growth of those tomatoes is plain to see, and through them you participate in life's renewal. Spontaneity, in the Hindu sense of the word, means being creative all the time.

What is particularly creative is to help another become himself. Creating does not just mean bringing a child into the world, it also means educating him. A mother is creative because she turns a baby into a beaming child and therefore into a future adult. Yet what makes human beings suffer nowadays is that they no longer "dance their lives," to use the beautiful expression of the celebrated dancer, Maurice Bejart. A craftsman felt creative when wrought-iron gates or earthenware pots were born from his hands, but most office work, even on a high level of responsibility, is not experienced as a joyful expression of one's vital force in an ever-new world.

A child spends his time inventing: he makes mud pies, he plays for the sake of playing, he is teeming with life. A child whose development has been impeded will later become a rigid adult, more dead than alive, cut off from his roots. Quite often, the child in you has lost his original richness. Because his maturing process was blocked, he keeps you from inwardly being your official age. So you will have to re-educate him, little by little, in order to bring him to the full stature of adulthood. And rightly experienced breathing during meditation will help bring back your inner creativity; it will also help you to become completely reconciled with sexual energy which is creative in the highest sense of the word but which, for most of you, remains associated with a certain uneasiness.

～··～

I am sure you will agree that one who is a prisoner of the past is no longer completely alive. In one who is completely and fully alive, the child has harmoniously disappeared to give way to the adolescent, the adolescent to give way to the young man, and the young man to the older man. There is beauty in the way one's life comes to an end. That was the case for Ramdas, who was so radiant and resplendent at the age of eighty-two that he was the envy of all.

If you restrain your evolution – even through a fear of growing old – if it is the child (and therefore the past) who continues to reign within you, then not only are you no longer creative, but you are no longer really alive. Live is movement; it is a process, a dance, an unceasing flow. And to be a prisoner of the past is to be under the influence of a certain number of psychological blocks which get in the way of life within us. These blocks can be sensed physically; energy no longer circulates in us and we cannot vibrate with it, we cannot follow the flow of life. In short, we cannot blossom.

What has hardened inside? The more life there is, the more flexible you are; the less life there is, the stiffer you are. The branches of a living tree are pliable, those of a dead tree break easily. A living body can move, a dead body is stricken with rigor mortis. The more flowing you are, the more alive you are. So let yourself feel handsome and regal in the meditation posture but do not feel as though you are made of stone, like a statue of Buddha or of an Egyptian pharaoh. If you do, you are dead.

Shiva's *lingam*, the phallus, the male sex in hard and rigid erection, cannot be a symbol of life because all that is hard and rigid is contrary to life. Although Hindu literature abounds in poetic images which imply that the male organ is the source of life – "the sex in erection from which a fountain of sperm emerges" – the truly alive attitude is female, not male.

An aggressive male attitude cuts us off from life. Still, as I have so often said, in the present world even women try to be male while men are afraid of their own femininity. Meditation consists in rediscovering one's inner femininity, both for a man and for a woman. In meditation, we become female; it is Dürckheim's "cup consciousness" which receives, just as the Grail received Christ's blood, instead of "arrow consciousness" which points toward its goal. Within the properly-maintained meditation posture which gives an appearance of rigidity, you become flexible again; you become liquid again like ice which changes back into water and flows with the river to the ocean. You cannot fuse with *brahman* – or with another human being if you dream of true love – if you continue to hold onto your own limited form.

Of course the role of the different psychotherapies is to let life flow again by making all that blocks it disappear. We therefore let out the cries we have held back or the tears we have had to swallow. The reason why *lyings* take such a harmonious place in Vedantic teachings is that they require a letting-go which gives us back our fluidity. Some of my readers who seriously practice the Tibetan path or do zazen have been put off by the idea of these *lyings*; they have concluded that Swami Prajnanpad was not a guru. They did not see how rich *lyings* are in the framework of Swamiji's teachings as a whole. (Or Denise Desjardins and I were not able to convey this to the public). In *lyings*, you start to flow once more. This also happens in meditation, even though you are controlling instead of expressing. To put it another way, in the sitting position, as you exhale while emptying yourself little by little, you "ex-press" by breathing out old attachments, *samskaras* and *vasanas*, which dry up and evaporate. Do not count only on the power of reliving spectacular experiences to bring you back to life and free you from the past. Rediscover the life inside you here and now.

The blocks are well-known: an event was extremely painful; you defended yourself against the suffering you felt; you tried to deny it; you suffered to be suffering. Suffering that is struggled against conceals a passive attitude, even if this sounds paradoxical at first. We submit to it and it puts us in the position of the victim. Some have settled into this stage. Passivity is often qualified as feminine but I prefer to give the word precious value rather than imperfection. This is a pernicious kind of block: you suffer, you take blows, you huddle up. But you are not adult in your suffering; you do not accept it and you are incapable of surpassing it to free yourself. The only way to surpass it is through acceptance, non-conflict and non-duality.

There are others who try to be active. They fight against their suffering just as much but instead of being victims they try to hit their opponent and their denial is expressed through anger or aggressiveness. Some are never angry, but that does not mean that they are sages – just that they remain stuck in the attitude of the victim. The child whose spontaneity has not yet been repressed shouts "I'm going to kill you" at his mother and throws his toy at her if she refuses to give him a third croissant; others, who have been brought up on television, yell "Bang!" while pointing two fingers at their Dad because in Westerns the opponent is eliminated with one "bang."

Some do not dare burst out in anger. I was like that when I was young. Naturally things "blew up" from time to time, but I rarely lost my temper. I thought that was good . . . and once I discovered spiritual teachings, I thought it was even better. But in fact, I had quite simply set myself up as a victim. "My brother is the victorious conquerer, I am the victim; life deals the blows and I take them." Then there are others who place themselves on the anger level; they are forever "in a flaming temper" – although that too is a block. One reaction is no better than the other: by being a victim you remain a slave to the past; you are just as much a slave if you are quick-tempered. Those who externalize their anger and end up considering that they are surrounded by enemies are prone to sudden illnesses like heart attacks or brain hemorrhage; those who adopt a resigned and passive attitude will be more subject to slowly-evolving illnesses, such as rheumatism or cancer. But someone with an irritable nature, who refuses to be pushed around and is always ready to attack, is just as rigid as someone with a sad nature who plays the victim. Life no longer flows freely in either case. At times there has actually been crystallization, based on fear and neurosis, creating a false structure which must be destroyed. Aside from all the other aspects of meditation, when it is accompanied by conscious breathing you find yourself little by little able to rediscover that inner life which is deeper than the role of the victim staggering under the blows or the hothead who tries to strike out at others to protect himself from suffering. For not beyond but at the root of this whole structure, which is the fruit of the past and keeps you from being creative, is life itself. And life remains forever intact, even if the make-up of our *psychism* progressively manages to cut us off from it.

The good news is that, before these psychological blocks come into being, not only is the ultimate (the *atman*) eternally unperturbed in you, but so also is life or energy (*atmashakti*) in you. If you feel the absolute to be somewhat remote, realize that life in you, the vitality which continues to make you breathe in spite of your respiratory blocks, is forever intact. It is renewed at each instant and nothing can contaminate it, like a spring flowing ever-pure but which would immediately be polluted if it came into contact with foreign matter.

I marvel at Saint Teresa of Avila's words to the conquistadors, who were then the glory of Spain: "Adventurers! Oh, conquerors of the Americas! Through efforts greater than yours, through sufferings greater than yours, I have discovered a world which is forever new because it is eternal. Dare to follow me and *you will see*." That little woman dared call out to the heros who were bringing back tons of Peruvian gold to the Spanish court. This ever-new and eternal world (to return to the sobriety of our own lives – we who are not Teresa of Avila) feels like a spring of life continuously bubbling up inside us. It can also be felt to resemble a beam of light from the bulb of a projector, shining out eternally transparent, a light which goes on to pass through a film and becomes colored as it hits the screen. Meditation is not only the inner search for the inexpressible, for that which is over and above everything; it is a way to connect yourself with this dynamic life source which is perpetually intact in you but which you perceive only as it has been filtered through the mind, through the *koshas,* through all with which you identify. No matter how imprisoned you are in the past, the life within you has never been affected; each second it is perfectly new and spontaneous – and meditation helps you to rediscover it.

Many have an idea of meditation that is inspired by the immobility of the posture and by terms like *atman,* absolute and Unmanifest. They consider it an exclusive search for the silence of an unrippled lake on a windless day. When a lake is disturbed by wind and little waves form on the surface, the water is no longer transparent and you cannot see to the bottom. Once it again becomes completely calm, it is limpid and clear; fish can be seen swimming in its transparent waters. If your mind is at rest, free from what are called the *vrittis* of *chitta* in yoga (great or small disturbances of the *psychism*), then reality around you becomes transparent and you gain access to what can never be described by words: the ultimate depth of reality. Meditation is thus considered to be absolute silence (and from a certain point of view, this is true): breathing itself slows down, at times one spontaneously holds one's breath and one discovers a consciousness free of all forms, an empty mind comparable to a blue sky or infinite space.

These are true images but they blind you to a first truth which will be much more familiar to you than this Emptiness, this Infinity, which is not something you can relate to right away. Meditation is not only the search for the Unmanifest within you, it is also the search for the manifestation or the dance of Shiva at its source, the energy aspect of reality (*shakti*), eternally intact inside you, the life force which is ever-new, ever-spontaneous, ever-creative, ever-renewed, never affected by the past. This approach may find more of an echo in you, indeed it is precious as far as your attempt to free yourself from the past is concerned. Otherwise you just wither away on the spot, like a tree which dies without bearing blossoms or fruit. No matter what fixations or psychological blocks you may have had in the past, inside you the screen onto which the film of your own particular fate is projected has never been touched. It is perfect here and now. And this eternal life never stops springing forth in you. . . but it keeps passing through the film, it is tinted, and once again you end up grappling with the same problems and prey to the same difficulties.

In meditation, do not just take interest in "that which is unborn, uncreated, devoid of aggregates and non-becoming." Return to the ceaselessly rising, ceaselessly bubbling fountain. Through the great inner silence and the suspension of ordinary functions, try to feel that you are eternally new, before the contamination of the past. Seek that "overabundant" spring of life described in the Gospel. It is this that allows you to blossom forth. And this spring which nothing can dry up or sully, in spite of former trauma or the wounds of your inner child, is there to be discovered. You need only go inward, as long as your thoughts and contradictory emotions are willing to quiet down for a while.

The depth waiting there for you corresponds to life without the dualities of happy/unhappy and good/bad. As Gurdjieff said, "A stick always has two ends." Everything that we have experienced is a stick which invariably has two extremities. If one is called success, the other is called failure; if one is called union, the other is separation; arrival/departure; health/sickness. But *atmashakti* in itself has no opposite. It is not beyond, but rather prior to opposites and dualities (*dvandvas*, in Sanskrit). *Atmashakti* is life in the pure state which goes on to express itself as yin and yang. If you can accept the whole of existence – friends and so-called enemies, good news and bad news – you will return to the fullness of life. It is not half life but full life which lets you feel non-dual life. This is the universal teaching. You can experience it more quickly than you think, if only you show a little perseverance.

But in the beginning, you will not immediately find this life on the heart level. Or if you find it too quickly, you will lose it. Many have known divine moments which have lasted only a few days or at most a few weeks. Whether you are a man or a woman, it is first on the gut level that you will find life. You will find God in your heart but it is in the *hara* that you will find yourself. Keep in mind the precious words of Karlfried von Dürckheim, reminding us that we Westerners have lost the sense of our abdomen although its importance was known to former Christianity, as the "Gothic belly" of medieval statues shows. This life, *atmashakti*, will reveal itself in your pelvis whereas you will find the *atman* in your heart. Ramana Maharshi reminds us that in order to indicate himself ("Who, me?"), a man instinctively touches his chest. It is true, I agree, that he does not point to his *hara*. The Self shines forth in the heart (*hridaya* in Sanskrit, *qalb* in Arabic, *coeur* in French), but one's vital force originates in the lower abdomen from which it never stops springing forth . . . even in solitude . . . even in hardship.

Since this source resides in you, each time you attempt to turn inward it is possible to become whole again and to feel the life expressed in your breathing and in the vibration of each of your cells. Being completely relaxed and motionless makes it possible to perceive this. It is possible to experience it this very day. You can obtain a distinct feeling of your muscles if you relax them, like in Schultz's autogenous training or in sophrology. In the Gurdjieff groups we also practiced many exercises based on sensation. If you are self-aware and completely relaxed, you become conscious of an unimaginable life in each cell of your body, as though you could feel your metabolism constantly at work. This is not an extraordinary accomplishment for which you must do a ten-year retreat in the Himalayas.

And why put things off? The mind specializes in always postponing things. If I am practicing meditation in order to discover life within myself, why can I not experience it right away?

It is not just a matter of orienting yourself in the right direction, it is a case of taking the plunge; the door is open . . . go out. As you know, what you thought was a serpent is nothing but a simple piece of rope; do not remain closed up in the house, go out into the garden! This is where fear often comes in: if I really become alive again, all my narrowness, all my petty habits will be carried away by the stream of life within me. So I wait, I postpone. "Oh that's for great yogis, not for me." We have the impression (to go back to the beginning of this talk) that if we are no longer tied to the past, if we rediscover the eternal present, we are betraying someone, we ourselves are going to stab the suffering child inside us.

And you remain that suffering child, even though you are given the opportunity to leave the past behind so that you can finally live in the fullness of the present, where every moment foretells a free future. No longer a fixed future, repeating itself indefinitely, but a festival of newness.

Try to see clearly what in you aspires to this freedom from the past, emerging onto a really new life and therefore a completely open future. And see too what in you refuses this transformation, what says "this is almost too good; I have no right to it because it would mean sacrificing my wounded inner child, the one I consoled by sucking my thumb and cuddling up in my own arms."

Imagine a woman, the mother of a family, who is unhappy with her husband and suddenly discovers true love with another man. She could think: "This is wonderful, but I have no right to it; I can't abandon my children or separate them from their father because they'd be too unhappy." You may feel a heartrending somewhat similar to this woman's, but in fact you are mistaken. "This is wonderful! . . . . But tomorrow, tomorrow . . . ." Why not now, since the fullness of life springs forth in you unceasingly? You are wrong in thinking that some duty forbids you this present fullness. What duty? "I am responsible for the pain-filled little child whom I have been consoling for forty years; I will not abandon it so I can be happy and fulfilled today." You are struggling within a contradiction which is all the more insurmountable because you do not clearly recognize it: you want a rich and ample life, but "later." Swamiji told me the stupid but well-known story of the sign in the barber's window saying, "Free shave tomorrow". . . always tomorrow . . . day after day, tomorrow. Of course it can always be "tomorrow"! Ask a mother to abandon her child! Even if you give her the best of arguments, arguing that it is necessary for her fulfillment as a woman and as a lover, she will refuse. Become aware of this inner contradiction; little by little, it is killing you.

The only real way of being faithful to that wounded child is to offer him life. Ever since he was born, he has wanted to grow and to blossom forth, to know the fullness of overabundant life. Give it to him: you will be giving him all he has always been waiting for and has never known. I felt this difficulty but I did not understand it as clearly as I do now, knowing each of you. I can say that today I even have the feeling that that little unhappy Arnaud that I knew so well never stops thanking me for giving him back the full life that he had lost.

Forgetting the weight of the past, of your *samskaras,* of the whole psychological level for a moment, let breathing take you by the hand and show you how to welcome *prana, ki*; let it show you how to open up to this energy. Another conscious breathing exercise, not as well-known as the *hara* one, consists in breathing with the entire surface of one's body as if it were permeable. You open up completely and let *prana* penetrate you, not only through your nose but through each pore of your skin. Breathing welcomes us on the threshold of the inner temple into which meditation conducts us, deeper and deeper. From there on, it no longer lets us go. It goes on to guide us to that very spring which is designated by the word "breath": *pneuma, atman.* If you give yourself to your breathing, it will lead you to the very heart of yourself, to the Holy of Holies. You can see that this no longer has anything to do with a physiological approach. Certain texts do indeed speak of *pranayama.* But they insist heavily on the physiological aspect, saying breathing brings more oxygen to the blood thereby intensifying mental activity, or it decreases brain irrigation and, consequently, mental chatter. A certain approach to *pranayama* is degrading to the sacred function of breathing. It is using this practice to embellish the ego, forgetting that breathing is the primary manifestation of God within us.

Since we base ourselves here on the heritage of Swami Prajnanpad, think of his words: *"Eating is a function of life; breathing is life itself."* Breath is the Holy Spirit for a Christian, *atman* for a Hindu, *ruh* for a Sufi. Always the spirit . . . the wind . . . breathing.

During your attempts at meditation, pay attention to a few technical details like your sitting posture and the way you hold your head but above all meditate with the feeling of the sacred, the feeling you would have if you were to meet Buddha himself. The greatest meeting of all is meeting one's inner self, meeting God in one's own heart or the *atman* in the "cave of the heart" as the Upanishads say. To get there, you need something to lean on; you need a method. Turn inward, go within, try to feel your essential being. For a few seconds you are moved; having reversed the direction of your attention, you find yourself again. But very quickly, distractions return; interfering thoughts carry you away. This is why there are many rather elaborate techniques. These techniques may differ in points but all right approaches have certain common denominators. You are preparing yourself for a tremendous discovery – a sublime revelation in your innermost heart, a revelation has not yet been given to you. And it will come about if you are guided according to certain traditional, coherent methods.

6

LIBERATING CHRISTIANITY

ALTHOUGH Hinduism, Buddhism and Islam (or more precisely, sages from these traditions) have held an essential place in my life, Christ, the Gospels, certain early fathers of the Church such as Gregory of Nyssa, and Cistercian spirituality were equally important.

But over the last twenty years, I have met and tried to understand many baptized persons disappointed in their religion, as well as a certain number of priests open to the psychological conflicts or even the tragedies in the lives of the faithful who are under their guidance. As for atheistic sociologists and psychotherapists, they make no secret of their harsh attitude toward what they call this "alienating religion," with its "oppressive morals." Practically step by step, I have personally followed the difficulties of some who are torn between the religious teachings of their childhood and the call echoed in so many books, magazines and television programs for a life which is "free" from complexes and inhibitions.

Christianity itself is actually a message of freedom, joy and love. It is in our own interest that it entreats us not to play the fatal game of licentiousness and – let us have the courage to say the word – immorality. "Man is not made for the Sabbath, the Sabbath is made for man," as Christ reminded us. Before condemning your own religion, put a little trust in a God of love who wants only what is best for you.

Swamiji often made the gesture of a closed fist unfolding little by little until the hand is completely open. This is a movement of expansion going from what is the most narrow to what is the most vast – a widening. It is simultaneously a growing and an opening – just as a bud opens and the flower blossoms. There is therefore a very close tie between these two ideas: growing (from the smallest to the most immense) and opening.

The word "opening" itself holds a meaning which can transform you from the inside, the more (so to speak) you open yourself to the very idea of opening. And there are different levels of opening: gross opening, subtle opening and spiritual opening. In the same way, there is the opening of the body, the opening of the heart and the opening of one's intelligence. "Closed-minded" and its opposite, "open-minded," are common expressions in everyday language. Closed or open to new perceptions, new ideas, new insights. How can you expect to grow if you remain closed? Because of its very dynamism, "opening" can be a key word on the way: it implies a moving forward and a richer future. A door is not simply open or closed; it opens little by little, starting off completely closed and ending up fully open.

It may be broad daylight outside, with the sun shining, but if we have closed the shutters and drawn the curtains, we remain in darkness. The sunlight really is there – we have not created it; we can only let it in. Yet we must open the curtains and the shutters for light to enter the room. We do not have to do everything by ourselves on the path; part of what is to be achieved lies beyond our power. If we were to rely on our own efforts alone, those very efforts would keep us within the world of the ego and the ordinary mind; they would not lead us to transcendence. At one point, a Reality which surpasses us comes into play. This Reality reveals itself as boundless and eternal, in contrast to ordinary states of consciousness which do permit us to feel infinite. So in a way, we passively let in the light when we open the shutters and the curtains. What else can we do but receive the light? But on the other hand, we actively open the curtains and the shutters. You must be very active on the path in order to get rid of the obstacles or, if you prefer, much effort is needed to arrive at the effortless state.

When we are not carried away by some worry, preoccupation or particular interest, we have a certain self-awareness. This awareness can only grow through openness and such openness works in two directions (at least this is how we perceive things initially): we open to what we feel as being inside ourselves and to what we feel as being outside ourselves. Our self-awareness can only grow if we open up. But it must be both an outward and an inward opening. It is possible to be doubly closed: closed to the outside and closed to ourselves. If we are closed to ourselves, we are cut off from our deepest roots, from our fundamental energy. This happens because of all sorts of mechanisms that psychologists study, like blocks, the separation between the conscious and the unconscious, and so on.

In fact, it is one and the same life which is at work both outside and inside us. Opening up starts from wherever you are right now. And if you want it to lead you not only to human fulfillment (which is the goal in psychotherapy) but also to spiritual fulfillment, you must start by admitting that the same unique life, the same unique reality, which animates the entire universe also animates you; you must admit that all that you become aware of – multi-faceted though it may seem – is the expression of an energy which is actually one, *one without a second.*

Hindus, you know, consider the whole world to be the dance of Shiva. The universe is God expressing himself. The usual Christian approach, however, is to see God as a creator outside of his creation – like a potter, a sculptor or a painter who is distinct from his work – while Hindus affirm that God is both transcendent and immanent, beyond and at the same time within his creation. If God is a creative artist, he is like a dancer who expresses himself through his dance. The universe is the dance of God – whatever meaning you may give to the word God. The important thing is to make the prodigious discovery that mystics have named God, Ram or Allah. All that happens is an expression of God. Whether you are an introvert or an extrovert, you can only find God or ultimate Reality through his expression, that is, through everything around you, including other human beings. The more you can open up, the closer you get to God.

Always open the door – it is always God who is knocking, even in the form of an enemy. Hence the words: "Love your enemies," "Forgive those who offend you," "Pray for those who persecute you." Always open up. Someone is knocking at the door, the door of your being. Always open up, it is God knocking. This is the ultimate Truth. But how can you little by little come closer to this truth?

If what is inside and what is outside emanate from the same reality, the only way you can really progress on this path of unfolding, like a bud that blossoms, is by being ready to open up inwardly and outwardly at the same time. Otherwise you cut yourself off from fifty percent of your possibilities for growth; you mutilate yourself. If you are unable to enter into contact with your inner life forces, with the *shakti* within you, you cannot open up to the outside. Here we enter into the domain of psychology and neurosis: if certain important tendencies, certain forces in you are blocked and repressed, the mind will remain tense, paralyzed by the inertia of your habits, and it will prevent you from blossoming forth. If you are incapable of welcoming what is within you, you will not be any more capable of welcoming what is outside you; life is thus no longer possible – neither human life nor spiritual life.

～ · ～

"If your mind lives, you die; if your mind dies, you live." To put it another way: if you open up, you live; if you shut yourself off, you die – even if you appear to exist. Opening up is directly linked to growth (which has to do with being), as opposed to accumulation (which has to do with having). If we were able to open ourselves with ease to the life or energy expressing itself in us, it would lead us to God. This is because man first perceives God through life and energy. All forms of life and energy are manifestations of God. This is a universal concept, found likewise in Hindu and Christian theology. Access to ultimate, unmanifest reality is gained through manifested reality.

Everyone has some idea of what it is that I am calling Life in us. For example, we can say that someone is very alive or that he is rather dead. Life is not a product of the intellect – far from it! Look at the life found in an embryo; in nine months, it turns a little cell born from the fusion of an egg and a sperm into a fully-developed baby, with lungs, a brain, a nervous system, a heart, arteries, veins and blood circulation. Life then goes on to make these organs grow. As the baby becomes a little child and the child becomes an adolescent, all those organs grow in size while continuing to function and to play a role that seems extraordinary, even if you are only a layman in physiology. Malformations aside, nature takes good care of things. We all started off with this prodigious life which turned an egg, the original cell, into a human being in nine months. Our mother had nothing to do with it. All she could do was not hinder the pregnancy process, taking care to avoid things harmful to a pregnant woman. We ourselves, as embryos, had nothing to do with it either.

This incredible life animates us constantly. But little by little, we rigidify it; we no longer allow it to be expressed in us. Nothing stops the *shakti* from expressing itself first in the embryo, then in the fetus and later in the creation of a baby; the embryo feels no particular fear of growing or taking form. The tragedy of human beings is that this abundance of energy little by little becomes blocked and divided against itself. It no longer goes solely toward expansion, intensity and participation in the life of the universe; instead, two breaches form. One breach, progressively accentuating with age, separates us (each of us individually) from the totality of the universe; this is called the ego sense. The second breach separates us from the life force within us; this results from repression, taboos and social necessities. And since our "no" –composed education is received unconsciously and is not felt as right, that very powerful life which we carry within us divides against itself. This is the meaning of the "Kingdom divided against itself" mentioned in the Gospel. Part of the energy continues to seek expansion and fulfillment while another part blocks, cuts off and represses inwardly. Consequently, we no longer feel that we are part of the whole; we no longer feel that the same life that animates the entire universe also animates us.

God is nothing other than the whole. You cannot have any real experience of God unless you have some notion of the word "totality." What does the Greek word *cosmos* mean? It means totality. You are part of that totality just as each wave is part of the totality of the ocean and you have a nostalgia for your infinite grandeur. One day the wave will be able to discover that it is the ocean and that all the other waves are also the ocean.

There is no point in holding a grudge against your parents, your teachers and the entire world. However it is important to feel what a personal tragedy it is that your own fulfillment has been checked and blocked so much. It starts when a child is told: "Stop it, do you hear? Don't shout like that! You're so annoying! Stop moving around all the time!" Then come all the other taboos that living in society makes necessary, until we reach the point where we no longer dare recognize certain mechanisms in ourselves. An energy block is formed as a result of repression; psychoanalysts call this the superego. Swamiji called it denial, the negation of what is, denying reality because of value judgements (like feeling that it is not right to make noise or that it is wrong to shout). Then little by little this repression becomes more complex.

There are certain general principles on which all psychologists agree, and then there is our own personal history. We no longer had the right to be and to assert ourselves. Here, I am using the words *to be* not in the metaphysical sense but in the very concrete sense of being alive and expressing oneself. The rhythm of nature has been inhibited. A tree has no complexes or inhibitions; parasites may be eating its leaves but it will still bud every spring. Unless they have been tamed or penned up in a zoo, animals express themselves spontaneously: peacocks fan out their tails, lions roar. In nature, we are the only ones who cut ourselves off from our fundamental energy. Imagine a ballet troupe with nothing but lame, crippled and half-paralyzed dancers. That is how human beings are. Look at the way birds sing and trees bud every spring! The more you progress, the more you will realize that the entire universe is divine. In certain higher states of consciousness you can even get a glimpse of the dance of atoms, electrons, protons and neutrons. The whole Universe sings God's praise and, into this ballet, a certain number of invalids have been introduced – human beings. This is both tragic and marvelous – because we have the possibility to rediscover our original face.

Each of us therefore has his or her own personal history and there are psychotherapies that help clarify why our energy has turned against itself. The conflict generally springs from the intervention of parents and educators, which we have internalized by means of a condemning process that says, "This is wrong." It is wrong for little girls or little boys to feel their own genitals, to touch themselves; it is wrong for them to be interested in certain things which awaken their childish curiosity . . . Adults react and you end up being cut off from yourself, with nothing but a small portion of your energy left to live with. A large portion of one's energy tries to express itself; a large portion ends up being used to stop this expression, and you have only a small portion left with which to struggle along.

Being a Westerner you live in a world which, while it clamors for emancipation, has not given you any real freedom. It is a world where the intellect has an exaggerated and therefore abnormal position. Everyone knows that in former times many Westerners did not know how to read and write although that did not stop them from being great craftsmen, like sculptors, cabinetmakers or blacksmiths. Later, all Westerners graduated from grammar school. Nowadays just about everyone has a high school diploma. To be a carpenter, it will soon be necessary to be brilliant in history, physics or chemistry. How will that make someone a good carpenter? A cabinetmaker does not need a head full of ideas, he needs intelligent hands. The predominance of the head gravely hinders our fulfillment. From a spiritual point of view, or even from a purely human one, the supremacy of the intellect is a mistake which has serious consequences. Look at all that encumbers our brain, from different kinds of reading matter (magazines, reviews, newspapers) to conversations with "It seems that this is true" and "It seems that that is true." Such abusive proliferation of thought estranges you from your vital forces and fetters your natural development. The profound destiny of man is not to remain where he is; man is not meant to be at a standstill. Too often, he withers away without ever having blossomed and grows old accumulating thousands of foreign ideas but without any experience of inner growth, which is his true vocation.

Because we are cut off from ourselves, fear has become established in us. Is it not terrifying to realize that we are afraid of the divine energy within us? Aside from those who are highly evolved, human beings are afraid of themselves. They are thus condemned to a fear of what is outside themselves because there is too great a risk that it will put them into contact with what is inside them. To bring outside and inside together into a whole, it is necessary to work in both directions, moving forward one step each day. Each obstacle you remove, each psychological block you do away with, frees trapped energy and lets your being grow. You must use everything available to rediscover this natural process of fulfillment.

For the moment let us assume that you have done one kind of psychotherapy or another and that it has more or less worked, so you take responsibility for your inner drives. The fear of what you are inside no longer dominates your life. You can therefore open yourself on various levels: physical, emotional, intellectual and sexual. This is the reality of nature. When there is an inner opening on the physical level, there is an effect on the sensation and motor impulse level; exercises of self-awareness and meditation let you begin to feel the life or energy that is there inside you. You also start to take into account your need to express yourself, to dance, to move. There is nothing mysterious about these initial realizations. But it is an enormous accomplishment to acquire a more subtle feeling of energy in its moving form or to feel your heart alive inside you. What keeps the heart from being alive? Sadness, grief, rebellion, aggressiveness. It is therefore necessary to do some methodical psychological work on oneself. On the intellectual level too, it is necessary to become receptive to the thoughts that come to us . . . without censoring them or stopping them from arising. This also means opening ourselves without fear to our sex drive. If you extend this initial and very simple state of opening farther and farther through all manifested – even the twisted manifested state of human beings – you will little by little open up to so-called supra-mental or mystical levels of consciousness. Would it not be terrible to miss the possibilities you carry inside and to lead a narrow life, when nature has planned such a rich life for everyone? Can you admit that the only time you were really yourself was during your mother's nine months of pregnancy?

It is absurd to believe that you can reach that great Reality within yourself without passing through the different stages of the Manifestation – the causal, subtle and gross planes. You will not attain the ultimate, brahman, God within you, the absolute, just by remaining silent. You must retrace the steps of the Manifestation – this is the whole idea of yoga. The unmanifest reveals itself on the causal, subtle and gross levels (*karana, sukshma, sthula*) and these three levels exist in you. To find God within, you must accept yourself since you are after all the manifestation of what is unmanifest, the dance of Shiva.

Everything in you is of God, even your feelings of hate. This is creation just as God made it. But creation is distorted in man because the mind smothers him and keeps him from opening up, causing inner division. You must strive – there is no other way – to pass inwardly through all the degrees of the Manifestation. An image I often use is that you cannot immediately take off your shirt without first taking off the pullover you are wearing over it. It is a question of progressively deeper layers. You cannot attain the absolute by denying the relative. I tried that for years. Only after Swamiji showed me that I had always come to a deadlock was he able to convince me to proceed in a more intelligent manner.

We can sometimes reach a state of unlimited consciousness that is nothing more than the play of action and reaction when we are up against life's limitations. This state of transcendent consciousness is technically called *samadhi*. It is a state that leaves us with an unforgettable memory. Still, it does not help us progress. Thousands of lives dedicated to spirituality have been ruined by the vain attempt to deny nature within themselves. One of the ill effects of education – even a religious education – is to deny life within oneself. Become alive again on all levels: intellectual, emotional, physical and sexual.

From the very moment you admit that you must become alive again, you realize – since life is one of relationship – that you are considerably cut off from the great Life by your ego sense. It is this latter which brings about the play of attraction and repulsion, desire and fear, like and dislike, and so on. If we are imprisoned in a separate ego, we no longer take part in universal life. Consequently, we must take the right direction to arrive at the goal set before us – effacing the ego – a direction in which you will win out both humanly and spiritually. Little by little you will come closer to a transcendent state that will give you a feeling of communion with universal life. Right now, how can you open up? If you admit that flowers, birds, other beings – always – are divine energy manifested, how can you narrow the closing (the closed shutters referred to earlier) that cuts you off from reality?

Our five senses are openings through which we receive all our perceptions which are then transformed into concepts or ideas.

Open up intellectually, try to listen to really new ideas instead of immediately rejecting them. Try to open your heart. (It is not an easy thing to do but we will come back to this later.) And open up physically. Some are physically closed, refusing sensations, refusing to perceive, refusing even to inhale. You will discover resisting forces in yourself, but who is going to gain the upper hand? If you have resolved to be stronger than your resistances, you are saved. And those of you who have a sex life, who do not transmute sexual energy solely through inner alchemy, open yourselves on the sexual level also – to participation, to sensation, to communion with your partner.

Everyday language abounds in expressions which show how much these ideas actually make up our human heritage, dating from a time when *being* still prevailed over *having*. For example, the words "open" or "closed" (to which Swamiji gave such great importance) can be found everywhere. Hindus use the words "closed" and "locked" in English. Do not try to open a locked door – first turn the key in the lock. Sometimes we do not really see the difference between things that are locked (which will be more difficult to open), and things that are simply closed (which can become open simply by a veritable decision on our part). You must try it, you must re-educate yourself as if you were a convalescent, you must learn to live again. And if you want to attain the highest states of consciousness, you must integrate all levels of the manifestation. Of course, important forces make us close up in spite of ourselves, so your conviction must be strong. Turning our five senses toward outside perceptions is relatively easy: we look, we listen, we smell, we learn to taste and to appreciate. Broaden your tastes. If Roquefort is the only kind of cheese you like, do not only eat that – branch out to other kinds. Open your ears to all sorts of music. God is in a Mozart symphony – this is often said – but God is also in the noise of a jackhammer, no matter how little your nervous system can stand.

"*Welcome*" was the word Swamiji used. If you say "welcome" to someone, you open the door to him. You cannot say "welcome" to someone while giving the key a double turn in the lock. Welcome to this perception, welcome to that sensation, welcome to what is new, welcome to what disturbs me . . . . Quite complex systems of denial and selection very quickly become organized within us. We totally drop the belief that it is always God knocking and we end up opening grudgingly, with the result that our inner growth becomes stunted. We impoverish the foods of impressions which come to us from the outside and which contribute to the growth of our subtle body.

In Patanjali's *Yoga Sutras*, the term *"pratyahara"* is translated as "taking away the objects of the senses." This gives the false idea that a yogi mutilates himself on the sensory level. And from there on, we come to the erroneous conclusion that we have to stop feeling. This is a totally false interpretation and counter to yogic tradition. Indeed, during rites – which are so important in India, Tibet and our Western monasteries – the five senses are actually used to encourage openness. Tibetans turn prayer wheels; Muslims touch the entrance to a mosque or mausoleum; Orthodox Christians kiss icons. Touch has a role to play in a rite, a liturgy or a *puja*. So does hearing – through bells, gongs, percussions, chanting, music. Incense appeals to the sense of smell. The decor, liturgical gestures, paintings and architecture appeal to sight. And taste also takes part with the intake of consecrated food – in the form of holy bread or the Eucharist in Christianity, or simply by what is called *agape* in other religions.

Agape, a very interesting word of Greek origin, means "refined form of love." The liturgy may seem cut off from life. But *agape* on the contrary – like the meal a Sufi master shares with his disciples or a meal brothers share in a monastery – fits completely into life.

The only way that you can open up is through the most magical word of all, the supreme mantra . . . yes. "Yes" is the translation of "*aum*" : the letter A – "yes" to Brahma, the letter U – "yes" to Vishnu, the letter M – "yes" to Shiva. Listening is the ear's "yes"; looking is the eye's "yes"; smelling is the nose's "yes"; tasting is the "yes" of the tongue and the palate; touching is the "yes" of sensation. The only way you can open up is through "yes." Someone knocks at the door, you decide to welcome him, you say "Come in" or "Yes." Refusing to open up is the same as saying "No."

The teachings that I am trying to pass on are wholly based on these two words. May you hear them today for the first time. "Yes" is the path of human and spiritual fulfillment, from the beginning level to the ultimate level, in perfect continuity. And "no" is always anti-religious. Of course I am not talking about times when it is necessary to say "no." If you order something specific and the wrong thing is delivered, you are right to say "no." The "no" I am putting into question is an attitude of inner denial which is never justified, like saying "no" to the rain, "no" to the clouds, "no" to the sun, "no" to human beings whose behavior I do not like. To say "no" is to say "no" to God.

Swamiji once gave me an exercise. (It is one that is also found elsewhere and so is not specific to his teachings alone.) It consists in sitting comfortably in a meditation posture or in a relaxed position and inwardly repeating the word "yes"; do not say "yes" to anything specific, and try only to feel that you are whole again. If you find yourself submerged by thoughts, it will not work. This apparently harmless exercise – simply repeating the word "yes" – can make such denial arise inwardly as to be almost unbearable. It is really interesting to see such a reaction. You can repeat the word either in a low voice or silently. Five or ten minutes of simply saying the word "yes" can transform your state of being, your level of consciousness.

The second exercise (and this one takes courage!) is just the opposite: "no, no, no, no." You can change your mood just by the power of the word "yes" and the power of the word "no." The word "yes" alone has an enormous positive, happy potential whereas "no" is enough to trigger aggressiveness. Merely saying the word "no" gives a tense, furious, ill-at-ease feeling. If you want to destroy yourself, there is no need to drink alcohol or shoot heroin, just practice this exercise! "No, no, no . . . " It will stir up unconscious memories which become more and more painful until you end up in an inner state that cuts you off, walls you in, stops you from communicating – just the opposite to a spiritual state. If you do not want to believe me, try it!

"No, no, no, no!" "Yes, yes, yes, yes!" There is unsuspected power in those two simple words. In all languages, the words themselves are very short: *ja, nein* in German, *oui, non* in French, *si, no* in Spanish. Unfortunately, the "no" exercise sometimes gives more immediate results than the "yes" one! There is so much repressed and crystallized denial in us that at first we find it easier to say "no" . . . "no" to Dad, "no" to Mom, "no" to our upbringing, "no" to toilet-training. The ordinary human being, the "old man" in us, is a walking "no." Emotional "no's" make the heart close up; physical "no's" cause contractions in the body (round shoulders, various tensions), and intellectual "no's" make you narrow-minded. The ego and the mind are directly associated with negation and denial. They have been formed and little by little rigidified by nothing but our "no's" . . . "No" to a certain way Dad acts, "no" to a certain way Mom acts, "no" to this, "no" to that . . . "No, no, no."

Of course, a certain amount of education has always been necessary to live in society, or rather – let us dare to say it – a certain amount of child-training. From there on, *the law* becomes established. Having gone largely into detail on that subject in a previous book, let me just add a few elements to shed light on what we are talking about today. From the Ten Commandments to the Hindu *shastras,* the law tells us how to behave toward others: do not kill, do not steal, respect your mother and your father. In actual fact, it commands us to do what we would naturally do if we had love. The law commands us: do not kill, do not hurt your neighbor. It demands that we do what we would be capable of doing if we were able to love. So the law ends up replacing love. This in fact is the tragedy of Christianity down through history.

To follow the Way is to rediscover love. From then on, love becomes the law. If you love, what you do is far more right than the very law itself. *Ama et fac quod vis,* love and do as you wish. You can be firm, you can punish, you can caress – all as a response from within. Yet we need the law because all human beings have not yet purified themselves enough to be able to love in the real sense of the word. I am not talking about infatuated love. So we have all been subjected to a law which has most often been badly presented by our parents, our teachers or those who have impressed us: "You mean to say you're interested in books like that? Just goes to show how much culture you've got!" A remark like that can inhibit an adolescent. The expanding to which I am beckoning you is a release from the law, from the training and conditioning of education – even if such training and conditioning are initially necessary in every society.

Original sin is nothing but the "no" that established duality, limitations and suffering. This is the way of iniquity. "Yes" is the way of redemption. That is why Christ can be called the attainment of amen. The story of Christ starts with Mary's "yes" to the Angel (there even exists a Notre Dame of the Yes) and it ends with Christ's ultimate "yes" when he said, "Be it done unto me according to Thy Will" as he submitted to his death.

Our "yes" to everyday life is a preparation for our "yes" to death. How can you say "yes" to death – which is the culmination of a fulfilled life – if you cannot even say "yes" to life? And how can you say "yes" to all the consecutive deaths which make up an existence, where Brahma, Vishnu and Shiva are constantly at work, where what appears disappears. . . how can you say "yes" to the death aspect of existence, if you cannot say "yes" to life inside you?

You have been taught not to say "yes" to the life force, to spontaneity, enthusiasm, movement, joy, expansion: "No, you won't express yourself, no you won't grow up, no you won't be fulfilled!"

And you have ended up making this "no" a part of yourself. Nonetheless, life remains intact and "yes" is the path leading back to it. It is a magic word. Both are magic words, "no" just as much as "yes" – but one will destroy you and the other will save you.

When I knocked at Swamiji's door, which was always open before my morning interview, he received me with "yes, Arnaud." He never said "come in" – just "yes" – and I felt that his "yes" was immense: Swamiji was saying "yes" to Arnaud as a whole . . . to Arnaud who arrived sometimes anxious, irritable, full of aggressiveness and fear for Swamiji, sometimes full of love for him. "Love your enemies"; that of course means say "yes" to your enemies. "Forgive those who have harmed you" implies say "yes" and understand. If we hear and we are moved, "yes" takes root in us and gives us a real desire to experience this growth which is both human and spiritual.

～・・〜

No matter how powerful it is, there is no "no" that can make sexual energy disappear. In the face of the energy within you, only "yes" proves right and it leads either to transmutation or to sexual intercourse. Transmutation means recognizing this energy, "being one" with it, without being "carried away" by it, saying an immense "yes" to it. This leads to a quantitative increase so intense that a qualitative change takes place. It is a law of nature. I am not saying that those who have no sex life cannot find God, I am simply saying that our sex life – which plays such a great role for the majority of men and women, married or unmarried – cannot be happy unless it is founded on "yes." And a very interesting and truly remarkable point is that this is an activity that nature has put at our disposal, in which the five senses can take part.

There are two human activities in which the five senses participate by saying "yes." One is the liturgy itself – as I explained earlier – and the other is the sex act as it was viewed traditionally, that is to say, complete and, to use modern language, daring. India has much insisted on the value of transmuting sexual energy and on chastity – chastity in the sense of modesty, not in that of having no sex life. A traditional Hindu woman would feel dishonored were she to arouse any man other than her husband. And yet that same India, like all the ancient Far East, placed enormous importance on eroticism. Vatsyayana's famous Kamasutras are not pornography; they are a genuine book of wisdom.

Sexuality is also this "yes" put at the disposal of nature as a whole: animals and plants have sexuality and sex offers human beings the joy of the simultaneous "yes" of the five senses. This of course means the mutual "yes" of the two partners, which can eventually apply to homosexuality. This latter is not in fact as categorically condemned by India as it is by traditional Catholicism; Hinduism just regulates it.

A human being can therefore only be happy by fulfilling himself or herself, by growing. We get a happy feeling from whatever represents expansion whereas retraction gives a painful feeling. This is the Way. Accumulating can give a feeling of dilation. For example, if you used to own a five-roomed apartment and have just bought a duplex with a thirty-foot long living room. Does one's sense of expansion come from accumulating possessions (even subtle possessions) or does it come from inner growth, with the closed fist becoming an open hand? This is the real issue. What spiritual teachings call real happiness, real joy, is not of course an accumulation of what you *have* but an unfolding of what you *are* in all domains: intellectual, emotional, physical and sexual.

But it is easier to talk about truths like this than to make them part of our life. A hardening has set in, firmly rooted in habits which have become second nature to us – with the tendency toward "no": "no" to our life forces (it is up to each of us to work toward his own resurrection), "no" to one aspect or another of reality. On the basis of this "no" to their own energy, human beings beg love. They live together for six months, end up disappointed, change partners, think they have found love again and are disappointed once more. This insatiable quest for love, constantly ending in failure, comes from the multitude of crystallized "no's" that have to be eroded little by little so that you can find your spontaneity again.

An important point – that so many of you who see therapy as the only solution refuse to admit – is that it is possible to say "yes" even if there are still "no's" remaining in us. Swami Prajnanpad's teachings cannot be summed up in *lyings* alone – and certainly not in past lives, fascinating though they may be for some. They are instead based on the ever-available opportunity that man has to conquer "no" by "yes." Draw back the curtains, open the shutters, let in the light.

What will gain the upper hand: your capacity to say "yes" or the force of the "no's" crystallized in you? Swamiji's path is an active one. "*He is a patient*" were the words Swamiji used to describe someone incapable of taking himself in hand. A disciple is a "*doer,*" one capable of acting and not just of crying and calling out for help. Swamiji also said, "*Give a little push.*" There is a little electric motor called a starter that gets the internal combustion engine of a car going and then the engine goes on running by itself. It is the same thing for you – you cannot always just sit and wait for someone to come to your aid. Why do you not want to give "*a little push*"? A doer capable of acting rises up against his machine status, his puppet status, and decides to say "yes" here, there, in these circumstances, to that aspect in others, to this aspect in himself. This enables him to open up . . . to open his heart, his soul, his spirit; it enables a woman to open her body to penetration by a man in a sexual relationship; it makes it possible to open up to another, to open up to everything. Believe me, saying "yes" in circumstances where you have always said "no" will be more liberating than *lyings*, until the time comes when you become "yes" because being "yes" means being alive. In his Second Epistle to the Corinthians, Saint Paul reminded the Christians, "Christ Jesus was not yes and no; he was only yes."

To be against life is to be against God; to be against Creation is to be against the Creator; to be against the dance is to be against Shiva; to be against the *shakti* – to use Swamiji's language – is to be against the *atman*. Denying the world under the pretext that it is not real is a futile attempt based on the misunderstanding that "all is Brahman, the film of appearances no longer interests me, I want to discover the immutable screen." Whatever your meditation techniques, you will never become established in the immutable screen if you deny the film being projected. For a long time, I tried unsuccessfully to do just that; Swamiji saved me from that mistake. Others tried just as vainly as I did, but no one saved them and they continued being afraid of themselves, afraid of life, afraid of creation, imagining all the time that they were going to attain to the unmanifest. You will not succeed on this false basis – or you might have "*a glimpse*" and then, on returning to your ordinary state, you will once more be carried away by the manifestation and by your refusal of the manifestation.

What does "God is in you" mean? How can you feel that God dwells within you? The first sign of God within you is your breathing. You breathe without feeling the need to breathe; "it" breathes; you do not breathe, Life does. Hence the importance of conscious and expanded-breathing exercises, sometimes combined with other forms of opening, which are found in so many spiritual techniques.

Remember: "Eating is a function of life; breathing is life itself." If, as it is, you dare discover that you are breathing and you let the movement grow, you will sense God within you. Sometimes our breathing changes naturally, according to our moods or the way we take part in nature; it is always divine energy at play in us. No matter how surprising or shocking it may seem, the changes in your breathing while you are making love are the *shakti* in you, they are God in you. Sufis say, "Islam is the expanding of the chest." What a beautiful definition! But most people say "no" to their breathing; they live with their lungs tightly closed within an undeveloped rib cage. It is said, "God is in you." "Prove it!" you answer.

The fact that your breathing goes on without your participation is proof right there. Life breathes by itself. What breathes in you? Universal energy. This is what makes leaves bud on trees every spring and this is what will lead you from the manifested back to the Unmanifest. By all means, do not let yourself become infatuated with creation, do not fall wildly in love with a woman and make her your whole world. That is idolatry. That is how nature makes you forget the Creator. Naturally if all you see is the dance, you will never see the Dancer; if you only see the creature (and the creature can be a flower or a human being, it can be the child you adore or the wife you love) then you will not see the Creator. It is always necessary to see beyond the manifested, so as not to identify with forms. To bow down before the Golden Calf is idolatry from the exoteric point of view, but technically, from the esoteric viewpoint, idolatry means turning something relative into an absolute. That is why we are told and retold again and again: do not attach yourself to what is manifested, changing, ephemeral and evanescent. Seek the ultimate.

Yet do not be led astray by teachings like this. Do not deny the Creation under the pretext that you are seeking the Creator. I mentioned earlier that some have come to the conclusion that to seek the ultimate they must turn their backs on the manifested; that is how they interpret *pratyahara* or yogic internalization. If this is so, why are ceremonies involving the five senses so important? And why is *tantrayana*, which among other techniques includes ritualized sex, part of esoteric teachings? Only through nature can you discover the supernatural, yet you must avoid becoming a slave or a worshiper of nature itself. Granted, if your whole life revolves around going to nightclubs and sleeping around, that will hardly lead you to the plenitude of the human state. But if you deny any aspect whatsoever of yourself, you are killing yourself and you are killing the Self. I do not know the Sanskrit for "killing God," but I do know the term for "crime against the *atman*."

The absolute is the relative, the relative is the absolute. "Emptiness is form, form is emptiness" according to Buddhist teachings. So let's apply these words to ourselves. God animates us but what have we become? I can still hear Swamiji's words: "*so miserable!*," "*crippled.*" This is how the majority of human beings are, like a shadow over Creation.

At times you have the right attitude: if you like to swim and if you swim without mind – just water, no thinking – you become normal, at ease, natural. There is no interference from the head, you are "yes," you are alive. Or perhaps you like tennis, so you play. You cannot "think" or you will miss the ball. For an hour you do not think, you are one with the ball. But you cannot spend your life swimming, playing tennis or singing, without thinking. Be alive, be real. Take part in Shiva's dance and you will become beautiful. Otherwise, sad to say, a human being cut off from himself is no longer part of nature. Sometimes we see faces that have become ugly – in the ordinary sense of the word – through lack of life and expression. We are not to blame. It comes from a closing up that goes back to our childhood, our education and the way we have reacted. What else could we have done but feel "no, no, no, no"? Our childhood "no" was nothing but a "no" of anger or despair. In either case, this breeds denial and negativity; later it is our job to dissolve our inner sclerosis so we can rediscover our spontaneity.

It is true that if, little by little, you want to disintegrate this armor of habits, rigidity and fixations (based on denial stored up in the form of *samskaras*), *lyings* can help you. So too can clear vision or understanding. But if you choose life, if you give "*a little push*" each time, it is also possible that life itself will be the stronger. I know that most of you find this difficult to admit: "Ah, until I relive my relationship with my father who . . . ." No, live! Live! Life is pushing up inside you. If you choose life, you are helping, if only a little. Say "yes" and life itself will shatter what is stopping you from being – as long as it is a wholehearted "yes."

Swamiji managed to convince me, although it was a difficult process because a large part of my Protestant education went against life. When you are six, making noise is wrong. When you are fourteen, sexuality is wrong. I was inhibited, stiff, ill-at-ease; I hardly dared breathe; I felt like I was suffocating – a suffocation which was created then and there at the age of two and was released by *lyings,* that is a fact. Yet one day Swamiji said to me, *"Father says it is bad, Swamiji says it is not bad."* He felt that this was something I could understand and those words certainly did have a strong impact on me. "You mean I can?" "Of course, Arnaud!" It was not a question of anything terrible but it did concern something I needed at the time and did not dare grant myself. It is always the same story: your father told you, "Don't do that; it's wrong." And if it was not your father, then it was your mother or a teacher or the first woman you met . . . . Psychological blocks are engraved in us at different ages, be it six months or twenty years.

Another time Swamiji told me, *"If it is a sin, Swamiji will go to hell"* because he is encouraging you to do it. All these words were liberating for me and I said "yes" to existence. Saying "yes" to existence does not mean giving in to reckless explosions of our vitality which is suffocating under inhibitions or fears. It does not mean "letting everything loose," having a ball or having a wild time. Such untimely outbursts of too-long repressed energy will get you nowhere. They are just a reaction to a feeling of unbearable suffocation and we let ourselves get carried away. Afterwards we are full of remorse and that condemns us to feeling even more inhibited the next day. How can you break your chains without unleashing your inner fury?

Instead of clumsily lashing out in reaction to your frustrations, choose to live, choose to expand. There is something you can do. Break down the "no's," the obstacles, by choosing "yes." There is great potential in this. Breathing will help you. Dare to breathe and you will open up. Dare to listen, dare to welcome, don't just live in fear! *Yes, yes, yes.* Someone is criticizing me, attacking me:

he is expressing himself. Do not judge, do not condemn . . . understand, forgive, love. Open the door to your heart lest you grow old without ever having lived.

⌣ · ⌣

"Yes," opening and love – these are the keys that open the prison door. You cannot love God if you do not love his creatures. Yet you cannot love others without first of all loving yourself. How can you expect to turn toward others if you are reduced to the tragic situation of denying life in yourself – as if it were wrong to have sexual desires, as if it were wrong to want to move about, make noise and shout? It is not wrong. If you become yourself once again, there will be a wisdom directing your actions. There will be an inner understanding of what does you wrong and what lets you blossom.

According to Genesis, God saw that his Creation was good. So is turning away from Creation to seek the Creator not mocking God? Why would He have made Creation if we were supposed to turn away from it? Use the Creation to seek the Creator. No lying to yourself. For you, today, the Creation is Mary, it is Peter, it is all of you. Where is God just now? He is here. I am not using grand phrases or some strange kind of mysticism here to give you the impression that I see things that you do not. If you refuse to see the waves, you will never be able to see the ocean. Where is life? It is here. Where is God? He is here – inside you, outside you. God animates you and God animates me; I see God in myself and I see God in you. Start on the most natural level possible, otherwise your spirituality will be neurotic and it will lead you nowhere. At least be natural – like a tree, like a bird. Dare to be natural. This will not always be possible in your job. There is no doubt that being a craftsman, using a tool or doing something with one's hands allowed people of the past to be more expressive than people today who do nothing but accounting or paperwork. But at least try to rediscover nature, even if this is something it is becoming more and more difficult to do. I was a teenager during the Occupation and there were no cars in France. You could camp out just about any-where; some people traveled the roads by bicycle, others would do twenty miles on foot, singing as they went along. Try to get back to a natural life – to an animal one even.

From the time of the caveman up until today, it is sex more than anything else that has helped man remain natural. What a pity sex is contaminated by the head, by fears, by prejudices and by inhi-bitions! Nature gave man sexuality as a great blessing, so that he would remain in contact with life. The whole of nature is based on sexuality. Flowers, for example, are the sexual organs of plants.

How terrible to see what the mind is capable of, making us so very perverted and distorted! Become normal again on the animal level, be alive, and that also means sexually. But the Way does not stop there. One woman told me recently, "I've come a long way sexually. I've had some really wonderful orgasms but that's just not enough; I can't believe that's all I'm destined for." Full growth as a human being is certainly not limited to a fulfilling sex life.

"All is sexual, all is bipolarity, all is the mating of opposites." This is a Hindu concept. The drive for life itself is always sexual, bi-polarized, made up of attractions that complete each other and desire to unite.

Friendship itself is sexual because both of those involved are seeking communion, even if there is no touching. You are always trying to communicate, to commune. It is sexual to go to a con-cert; it is a coming together in which there is an opening up and a receiving. Opening oneself, receiving, even on the highest level, is always sexual.

This natural life then takes on a higher form. It is no longer a communion on the level of senses and sensations, as in swimming, playing tennis, making love or smelling a flower. "Love the Lord your God with all your heart, all your mind and all your soul." It is a blossoming that leads to a flowering of the heart and to Love. Making love well always leads to a higher quality of being. If you are really fulfilled sexually, you will see that sex loses importance of its own accord and is replaced by love. Communion no longer takes place through the five senses, instead it happens through the heart. In opening up, I am enriched. But it is my being – not my having – that is enriched. The love of the heart is another form of communion in which the senses play a lesser role. You cannot however oppress your sensuality and think it will fulfill you on the heart level. A shortcut like that ends in failure. Where it was once physical orgasm, the most perfect form of union between a man and a woman now becomes union on a soul level. This kind of purified love grows unceasingly within the fullness of "yes."

You start by loving your wife or your husband and your children, and your love goes on progressively widening, purifying; it becomes less and less selfish. Pure love takes root in "yes." But how difficult it is for this to be a real "yes," even with the woman you love, even with your own son! If you reach a love for your fellow creatures that is a true "yes," then your love for Creation changes levels and turns into love for the Uncreated. We no longer feel that we are in communion with one aspect or another of Creation but rather with Life itself or, if you prefer, with God. Classic Greek had three words to designate the different levels of love: *eros, philia* and *agape.*

Originally, religions always tried to consider us as complete beings who participated totally in existence so as to allow us to live fully and blossom. A harmonious sex life was sanctified by a sacrament like marriage. The original principles of religions did not just aim at oppressing us! Through the heart, we enter into communion with what is called the subtle level in India; when this level is experienced in a perfect way, it leads naturally to the spiritual level. I know of certain Hindu mothers, brought up to believe in the sacred nature of motherhood from an early age, whose love for their child led directly to love for God. They picture their child as being the young Gopal (Gopal was Krishna's name as a child) and their love for the child becomes so pure that it turns into spontaneous prayer – a communion with God beyond the gross, and even the subtle, manifestation. You then feel that you are no more in communion with the Manifestation but with unique infinite energy itself, the whole. I am the wave and I am the ocean at the same time because if a wave is in perfect communion with another wave, it discovers the ocean.

We can refine our love for our child, our wife, our husband, our best friend, by giving "*a little push*" to say "yes" to them. And we can do the same with our "enemies." Why should it not be possible to open one's heart? If you do not like this person and you cannot stand the sight of that person, you will never find God nor will you find the kingdom of Heaven within you.

In ancient Hindu society, love that became more and more purified and communion with life itself developed from a natural movement. If you discover life which surpasses the ego, you will no longer dream of saying, "It is my life" but instead, "It is Life." From then on, you will no longer fear death. What is born, dies. "My life" will die when I die, but "Life" cannot die. Life animates you and life is eternal. Once you are free from the fear of death, you will know the perfection of feeling no fear, the perfection of love, the perfection of communion.

But before that, you must follow a *natural* path and, as I so often insist, you must be normal before aspiring to what is supra-normal. Many people did not understand why Swamiji, who lived in strict chastity, took such pains to help someone who was sexually neurotic become sexually normal. Nor did they understand why he showed such love for our wounded dispositions. If Swamiji took the trouble to re-educate us completely, it was always in a spiritual perspective. But how do you expect to discover the Great Life if you do not take the responsibility for *your own life* in all its dimensions? Spirituality that turns into a compensation for our abnormality is spirituality which is bound for failure.

One who is free – like Ramdas who abandoned *everything* at the age of thirty-six to give himself to Ram – is not abnormal. I am not abnormal because I no longer roller-skate, even though my life revolved around roller-skating between the ages of ten and thirteen.

Certain aspects of your existence may fall away freely, but unless you completely fulfill your life in all its aspects, you cannot discover Life. A crime against *your life* is a crime against *Life,* and therefore against God who expresses himself through Life. This is why Swamiji so often said, *"Be normal, become normal again"* like uninhibited little children, overflowing with life. *"Open, widen, flower."* When Christ cured the deaf and dumb man, he murmured, *"Effata,"* open yourself.

What I have just said is in fact an ancient truth but I would like you to feel it intensely alive inside you – and alive is indeed the word. In many religious traditions we find the idea of inner rebirth, summed up in the words, "I was dead and I came back to life." This is the case for the Resurrection of Lazarus in its esoteric sense. Certain mystics – knowing that Lazarus' death had been officially pronounced, that he had already been wrapped in graveclothes and had begun to give off an odor – were wary of the literal interpretation of that passage of the Gospels. What is the point in a dead man's coming back to life so that he can die twenty years later? For one who seeks the ultimate secret, the essential lies in the discovery of that which cannot die, not in the temporary resurrection of a body. This account of a dead man coming back to life is a spiritual message. Lazarus is dead and Christ tells him, "Come out of your tomb, arise."

When I was with Ma Anandamayi and afterwards with Swamiji, I felt that that phrase was meant for me, just as it is meant for each one of you, "Arnaud, come out of your tomb." Christ gives life back to human beings who no longer dare to live, who seem to be at death's door. This is the meaning of Jesus' miracles, making the deaf hear, the blind see, the lame walk. Even if these miracles did actually take place, mystics and esoteric tradition do not limit themselves to such restricted explanations. What is important is this: how can Christ make you hear, if you are deaf; how can Christ make you see, if you are blind; how can Christ make you walk, if you are lame? This applies to all teachings, either non-dualistic or religious.

Swamiji brought me back to life on all levels, but being able to rediscover life is something that concerns every human being. For me, this image of Lazarus wrapped in graveclothes is a very explicit symbol: you are stiff, you are dead, smothered by the shell of the mind, by fears, false ideas, traumas, illusions, "no's." "No, you don't have the right to live, you don't have the right to love, you don't have the right to breathe, you don't have the right to move, you don't have the right to express yourself, you don't have the right to exist, you have a right to absolutely nothing." And the guru tells you, "Take off your graveclothes, arise, come out of your tomb, come back to life as Lazarus did." Yes . . . opening . . . growth . . . love.

7

HAPPINESS, GRATITUDE AND LOVE

WHY do we turn more toward spirituality and prayer, why do we think of God more often when we are in difficulty and suffering than when things are going well? God, in His love and compassion, makes us undergo affliction because "tribulations" purify us and bring us closer to Him. The saints have all borne witness to this. Still, you do not have to take a dualistic religious perspective in order to look into the essential issue of how fervent or how half-hearted you are on the path.

Buried within us is a profound wisdom, "*prajna*," the greatest wealth of our personal unconscious. This wisdom, which I call "the great unconscious," attracts whatever trials we need in order to progress. When we finally see clearly into our own unconscious and into the way we have functioned up until now, we realize what a blessing this is.

In itself, attracting misfortunes is definitely not a blessing. But it *is* a blessing for one who knows how to see, to accept and to go beyond the surface of life, for one who – in the very heart of adversity – discovers a peace and joy which others find incomprehensible. Yet there is something that is even more difficult to accept: to make real spiritual progress, you must be happy. At first appearance, at first sight, we feel suffering makes us progress. A deeper truth, one more difficult to attain, is that happiness makes us progress. It is not easy to be happy and it gratifies us to hear that we evolve through suffering. What is more, if we are desperate and someone comes along and says, "To progress spiritually, you must be happy," our fate seems doubly cruel. The widespread belief engraved in us, that "liberation comes through suffering," is a betrayal of the highest truth. The highest truth for someone who shows subtlety, intelligence of the heart and skillfulness on the path, is that we make much more progress by being happy. But what kind of happiness does this entail? Happiness that just distracts us and gives us the impression that we are no longer progressing cannot be real happiness.

Swamiji hardly ever used the word "bliss" with me, although it is a very common word in India where the "bliss of the Self" is often mentioned. Swamiji always said "*happiness*." And one day when I used the word myself, he interrupted me saying, "*You don't know what happiness is*" – even though my life was giving me much satisfaction, much success and a lot of what dreams are made of. After years of difficulty, practically everything was finally being given to me. "*You don't know what happiness is, Arnaud.*" And happiness is not only the bliss of Buddha or *samadhi*, it is simply feeling happy.

All mystics try to share their discovery with us: happiness does exist but it can only be found in God. If we do use that word, with whatever meaning you want to put behind it (be it a pantheistic God, a personal God, an impersonal God, an ultimate God, the Deity), God is the pinnacle of happiness, the only absolute happiness. My own personal experience and conviction confirm this.

But first, what entitles us to speak of "God"? Revelation itself, even if you accept the idea, was passed down through men. Now maybe those men were raving, letting what they were projecting and imagining run away with them. In that case, their words have no value. Then again, maybe those men had a knowledge of what they were proclaiming. If that is so, then it leads us to the conclusion that God is an experience available to man. Some philosophers say that there is no God, that theology is nonsense and that religion is a childhood illness of mankind. Now either those philosophers are right or else those who spoke of God did so because they had "realized" Him, even if their experience was called a "revelation," because it was a revelation they themselves had embodied.

This prompted Swamiji to make a statement that shocked me at first because of my former Christian background. He said: "*God is the highest possibility of man.*" But I let it sink in. And now I agree. All theology affirms that Jesus Christ was 100% man. Jesus Christ was not 50% man and 50% God; he was 100% God and 100% man. So at least one man knew what he was talking about. God is the highest possibility of man – and that is true for all of us. A sentence like that has much more impact on us than picturing an inaccessible God in a faraway heaven. But how many men come near this possibility? It is a possibility that can be summed up in two well-known words which eventually merge into one: love (. . . but what kind of love?) and happiness.

This happiness must be taken in a totally new way. Being happy is the pinnacle of spirituality, even though in ordinary happiness we tend to forget awareness, to stop putting the teachings into practice and to let ourselves get carried away . . . until things go wrong once again, awakening our aspiration to suffer no more, to avoid emotions and to find a reality that provides a solution to all our problems.

The highest spirituality emerges from happiness – not suffering – because God is love and happiness; to use the supreme word, He is "bliss." And how could suffering culminate in supreme happiness? Ultimate happiness arises from the culmination of joy. We know that we have made progress on the Way, real progress, once we start feeling, "I am happier." But what kind of satisfaction does this imply? Happier as a wife, as a mother, as a musician, as the owner of a nice house. Only the mind, only blindness, makes us endow suffering with false value. Suffering is sometimes necessary; it is part of our path and we must undergo it to clear the way and attain happiness. But if there is a mistake in judgement or understanding – a kind of stupidity of the heart – we end up linking spirituality with suffering and linking happiness with the materialistic world. This approach turns all joy in life into materialism and selfishness: eating, drinking, sleeping and screwing. Sea, sex and sun – the "Three S's" of Club Med.

I am not saying that Club Med is the apex of spirituality but what I am saying is that wherever happiness reigns, God is expressing Himself. If you carry psychological knots or wounds inside, you will find these words difficult to accept. If someone says, "Getting up in the middle of the night and standing there with your arms outstretched in the form of a cross is the highest form of spirituality" – you will not consider that ridiculous. But to say that happiness is the highest form of spirituality . . . No, there is something wrong there. Arnaud is mistaken; that is pleasure-seeking, it is sheer hedonism.

Heartless though it may sound, it is the truth. If you are really honest, you will admit that all you want is to be happy. So why lie to yourself? I would like you to feel the grandeur that the word "happiness" took on when it came from Swamiji's lips. *The sage is a happy child.* One day, I heard Ramdas cite Aurobindo's famous words, "God is an eternal child playing in an eternal garden." As Christ said, the sage "has become like a little child again." But how unfortunate that those words have become so familiar that they have lost the wealth of their meaning! They are terrible words to hear. And just where do I stand in relation to that *"happy child"*? I am a poor miserable adult – and here, the word "adult" is used in its most ordinary sense: one who has lost his childlike grace, freshness and innocence, who is no longer capable of pure joy, who complicates everything, who sees pain everywhere, who is afraid to be happy and, to top it all off, actually goes back to sleep once things get better.

Let me share with you another very important expression of Swamiji's: *"heartfelt gratitude."* Gratitude is the first real feeling that gives birth to faith, hope and charity. Faith is not faith unless the heart takes part. And hope gives us the promise that "Ultimate reality is light, not darkness." On days when the sky is grey, it reminds us that the sun has not disappeared forever. I suggest that, in the first place, you discover this ever-so-precious feeling of gratitude. It is the opposite of frustration. Adults are not happy children playing in an eternal garden; they are frustrated children, repeating "I've never been loved enough, I've never been appreciated enough, I've never been given enough." At a time when others actually envied me, I remember Swamiji's words, *"When Swamiji saw that you were so miserable . . ."* That is the same thing Christ said, "You are whited sepulchers." There we are, smiling and good-natured, but what is behind it all? Suffering! To be really happy means just that – to be really happy. Being happy in itself will make the essential feeling of gratitude grow in you – a feeling without which no path can go far. It is gratitude that opens the way to love. It was gratitude that, one fine day, made love for Swamiji arise in my heart – real love, instead of my former ambiguity, somewhere between a need for him and a fear of him.

Do not misinterpret the word "love." A Tibetan once told me, "There is no greater love than a hunter's love for his game." And he added, "Such is an ordinary disciple's love for his guru." Indeed, a hunter will trek through the snow all night long to shoot his beloved deer. What love! He thinks of nothing else. And the disciple feels the same way toward his guru. At first he thinks, "I need him; he must give me what I need. I am going to use him." Well and good. But is there some new element that will little by little change our heart, open our heart? In the most spiritual sense, it is gratitude. And how are we going to feel grateful – not just to our guru, but to ourselves, to life, to fate – unless we are happy at last? Gratitude towards life is the first real feeling. The rest are nothing but inventions of the mind which will never satisfy you and never constitute a path toward freedom.

How can you feel gratitude when you are suffering? You will only feel gratitude for your sufferings if they have guided you to a quality of happiness that you have never before experienced. There is nothing intelligent about not being happy. Everyone wants to be happy. So people are not really very intelligent since they do not discover the secret of happiness. Absolute happiness, ultimate happiness, non-dependent happiness is not the only kind that exists; ordinary satisfactions can bring you truly unshadowed joy if the spiritual element comes and lights them up. It is just simple happiness that I am talking about. We are so afraid to be happy – because it may not last, because it is wrong to be happy while others are suffering . . . What selfishness! How can my suffering lessen the world's suffering? This habit of suffering has created in you a whole set of opinions or false ways of looking at things. You want to be happy and at the same time you do not consider that you have the right.

If God is man's highest possibility, man's highest possibility can only be the summit of happiness. Do not be afraid. Be happy. And take the idea out of your mind that there is a definite connection between spirituality and suffering, but not between spirituality and happiness. Happiness is ordinary, it is human, it is for everyone. For everyone? How unfortunate that it be for so very few!

There is a link between the words "happiness" and "recreation." Happiness constantly re-creates us. The incredible thing is that because of our abnormal, neurotic inner patterns, we feel that we exist when we suffer. But "to exist" in its etymological sense, "*ex-stare*," means to go out of oneself . . . to go toward expression, toward the manifestation. If we each exist as a manifestation of God, to live is to be happy. Otherwise, there is something wrong. The mind is interfering in some way. Sages are happy people. And, as he gets happier, a disciple progresses. It is not right to want to consider happiness nothing but on the level of mystical, supreme happiness. If you do, go off to a hermitage or become a great Carmelite like St. Teresa, the Little Flower. But even nuns in convents know how to laugh. Terrible though it may be, difficult though it may be – it is being happy that is beautiful, noble, religious, mystical. But do not confuse this with being stupidly euphoric; it is not possible to laugh and dance all day long on the pretense that you are celebrating the joy of life.

Why do we feel that ordinary happiness puts us to sleep instead of bringing us closer to God? Because we do not really feel gratitude. Does the following situation not seem strange? "I'm fine these days, things are going great; I'm putting the teachings much less into practice because everything's fine . . ." All right, suffering has not caught you by the throat. Suffering also can be a blessing if it becomes a passageway to understanding, allowing you to be happy in a new and different manner. Happiness that turns you away from God and from the Path, making you less motivated for spiritual practice, is mediocre happiness, dead happiness. It is not happiness. It does not give birth within you and it does not nourish a feeling of gratitude toward life.

When we feel grateful, we come closer to God. Even if you do not use the word "God," even if you discard the idea of a personal God as Buddhists do, you come closer to light, to the whole, to universal energy, to love. The natural way of progressing is by becoming increasingly happy, and thereby feeling increasingly grateful. Gratitude is the normal, natural path; the rest is the perverseness of the mind. Gratitude leads to love. But not to demanding-love, like a hunter's love for his game. Do not confuse begging-love with fulfilling-love; the latter springs from gratitude. And how can you feel grateful if you are frustrated? You are unable to feel grateful to life, to fate, to the world, but above all, to yourself . . . yes, grateful to yourself. You know that you do not love yourself and this is the root of the problem.

We do not love ourselves because we have not been able to make ourselves happy. Ever since childhood, we have been a cause of suffering for ourselves. When I was about six, I overheard some grown-ups talking about how beautiful they found my cousin's blond curls. There was no getting away from the fact that my own hair was straight and black – period. And how it hurt me not to be the one to receive those praises! How could I love myself? I could not forgive myself for having such hair. What is more, I was very skinny – I had no muscles and could not even scramble up a climbing rope; I was hopeless. I could not forgive myself for that either. I spent my childhood judging myself, refusing myself. And to compensate, I had to exaggerate the few points that let me love myself. A pattern like that makes one vain and self-centered. It is actually so simple. The harm does not come from loving yourself too much, it comes from not loving yourself at all. The most divine feeling you can have is gratitude to yourself, the feeling that comes when you can say : "I've managed to make myself happy instead of constantly letting myself be drawn back to what makes me suffer."

One day I really did thank Swamiji – even though "thank-you" is never said in traditional India so that one will find a more original, more personal way to say it. But since I was accustomed to speaking like a Westerner, I said, "Thank you, Swamiji." It was a sincere "thank you," not a half-hearted one. He answered, *Thank yourself, Arnaud.* For a moment, I did not understand. Then, not with the head but with the heart, I felt what he meant: "Swamiji has made you happy? Then thank yourself for having come to the ashram. Thank yourself for staying instead of leaving at the first difficulty. Thank yourself for having listened to Swamiji instead of answering 'yes, but . . .' as soon as he opened his mouth."

Gratitude toward yourself – that is one of the first religious feelings that you can experience. That is not selfishness. It is when we cannot love ourselves that we are condemned to self-centeredness. And love for yourself – not vanity or pride, but real love – is born from gratitude: "I have finally been capable of making myself happy."

If a stroke of good fortune comes to you from the outside, how have you managed to attract and receive it? On the one hand you attracted it and on the other, you received it. We sometimes attract some grace, some blessing from life, without being able to receive it; it is given to us, but we do nothing with it. Of course if you receive happiness from the outside, there is at the same time a fear of losing it because this "other" can take away what he, she or it has given you; you find it difficult to feel your present joy completely. You cannot really count on anything. Human happiness can always betray us, because karma – the chain of cause and effect – is at play. The one who loves us most might die. This is why every happy moment should be illuminated by spirituality.

The Way takes all that is relative into consideration. And it will lead you beyond the relative . . . to non-dependence, to the discovery of the Self. But to attain what you are seeking – the absolute, joy, peace, non-dependent plenitude – what is the method? Letting yourself blossom forth. This will culminate in an unwavering feeling of gratitude and love: love for yourself, love for your neighbor, love for life.

⚬ ⋅ ⚬

It is true that there is a certain way of being happy that brings our spiritual practice to a standstill. For days on end, we forget. But I must underline that unconscious happiness does not give birth to a real inner feeling of gratitude. I have nothing against Club Med; it is the picture of ordinary happiness: you spend two weeks in the sun, you feel great, you smile at the woman you love, people are friendly, the food is nice. Two weeks go by during which you are, in fact, happy. But is the religious feeling of gratitude not missing? That is where the difference with Swamiji's "happiness" lies.

This feeling of gratitude is lacking because you are not yet happy enough. And in a Club where everything is great, you will realize, "I didn't think of the Path even once in two weeks." Good for you! Sleep, seek ordinary pleasure and rest. But afterwards, you can move on to more, infinitely more . . . You can move on to consciously-experienced happiness. This is where the fundamental difference Swami Prajnanpad emphasized between *bhoga* and *upa-bhoga* comes in. *Bhoga* is generally translated as "enjoyment." Sometimes the word "indulgence" is used, but this latter is not *bhoga,* it is *upa-bhoga.* There is no true feeling involved; it is as if

157

you were not receiving anything. There are those who talk so much while eating that they do not even see what is on their plate; at the end of a meal, they do not even know what they have eaten. With *upa-bhoga* (ordinary happiness), you are carried away, there is no conscious appreciation . . . and therefore no conscious gratitude.

I can assure you that if this feeling of gratitude does not intensify by itself, it is because you do not really dare to be happy. When will you dare to be happy? I realize that it is possible, even probable, that fate still reserves you a few blows. My daughter Muriel's baby died. Such things do not only happen to others. I cannot promise you that your little son will live until eighty. Never compare your destiny with that of another. But take this seriously, it is important: how are you going to make yourself happy? Don't tell me that for you there is only one way to be happy – by becoming a recluse and meditating in your cell. But being loved by a famous star or giving autographs to fans on your way out of the biggest Paris theater will not fulfill you either – even though happiness can take on a very concrete, human form. Be careful of infatuation and be careful of what is purely neurotic.

Swamiji taught us to be happy. Part of his role was similar to that of a psychotherapist: he took care of our wounded hearts, not only through *lyings* but also through the talks we had with him. He helped us rid ourselves of the curse we have all crystallized into a well-organized system so we can make ourselves keep suffering in one way or another.

One day I dared say to myself: "I want to be able to be happy," not to have *samadhis*, as I had dreamed of until then. "*Be happy.*" Do I feel the heart of a child within me? Am I really serene in my day-to-day life and in my life as a whole?

Frustration will get you nowhere. Ordinary happiness, without the feeling of gratitude, will not get you anywhere either. Everyone has some experience of how his or her own mind works, of his or her own difficulties, main psychological knots, fears and inner twists and turns. But we remain unaware of the dimension feeling fulfilled contains. It is a mystical feeling. And that is as difficult for each of you to hear as it was for me. "I want what is grandiose; I don't want little human joys." We are on this earth to be happy. God is happiness, because God is absolute security. If you have discovered God in yourself, if you feel loved by God, sustained by God, carried along by God like a wave is carried along by the ocean – that is the ultimate accomplishment. And you will find God through love, you will find love through gratitude and gratitude through happiness. God is that non-dependent happiness that subsists through betrayal, trials and failure. On the surface, *karma* will continue. *Ananda,* bliss, is the ultimate reality of our being. It is man's highest possibility, which a few sages, a few saints, attain in this life. It is both love and joy: an ocean of love and an ocean of joy.

Dependent human happiness will lead you to non-dependent serenity. Can you hear that? . . . Happier and happier, happier and happier . . . Swamiji died at the end of 1974. In September, 1973, I was at last able to tell him: "I am beginning to dare to be happy," knowing what an important stage that was in his eyes. Could I have told him anything more precious? It is not man's sadness that praises God. To be happy in the midst of what others call suffering is the supreme accomplishment of life. How will you manage it? No one here is a second Saint Francis of Assisi or Saint Teresa of Avila. So how are you going to be really religious? Gratitude is the first pure religious feeling. And it will come when you dare to be happy with no background limitations.

Have a nice piece of Camembert cheese and a good bottle of wine, if you like that sort of thing. That is spirituality. One day you will no longer need even harmless little pleasures like those. "Thankyou" for what life gives me; "thank-you" for what it does not give me. In the meantime, the most "material" happiness proves to be spiritual if you are grateful. If you dare to see self-reconciliation through to the end and to rediscover the childlike soul within you, your whole heart will give thanks. You will be able to say, "What a wonderful evening that was!," even if you only spent it laughing at a Marx Brothers film. Everything will become religious once everything becomes happy. Many tell me, "I would like to lead a life of love." You are putting it wrong, "I would like to feel less self-ish" would be more right. Some have progressed enough to feel, "There is no love in me – or only a hunter's love for his game; 'I love' means 'love me,' it is begging."

I too suffered because I was unable to love as Swamiji loved, as Ramdas loved, as the saints loved. Suffering of that kind has precious value. But how can I manage to love? How can I open my heart? You start off immediately using the word "love," but "gratitude" should come first. It is impossible to love without gratitude. It is much more beautiful to love than to be loved. You will all accomplish it, if that is what you want. It is not too difficult for you to adore your handsome little son. But how can you feel real love for everyone, even those who are unattractive or difficult to get along with because they are suffering? You will not attain love without a huge "thank-you" in your heart.

What Christianity calls "thanksgiving" is an expression of gratitude, but it must come from the heart. If you are unhappy, it is useless to sing Daniel's canticle: "O ye lightnings and clouds, praise the Lord" or that of St. Francis of Assisi. God's people show their gratitude by praising Him. But what kind of gratitude are you expressing? "Oh God, we give you thanks for all your blessings" betrays a sort of plea that means, "Oh God, how wonderful it would be to be happy, let us pretend that we are." I recited prayers like that every Sunday when I was a boy. But truthfully, without getting carried away by our imagination, how can we begin to feel gratitude? And what stops us from being happy? . . . The weight of the past, psychological knots, fears, false ideas (which is why *chitta shuddhi* is necessary); . . . And a powerful mind (which is why we try to destroy or dissolve the mind – *manonasha*).

How is it possible to feel gratitude when you are leading a life of frustration? Since life is not necessarily going to give you everything, at least learn to appreciate with all your heart what it does give you. Then start off in quest of a happiness that will light up all tragedies. God is carrying me in His arms, like a mother carries her baby. If you do not accept the word "God," call it "*Shakti*," the "Divine Mother," "Universal Life," whatever term you like. This discovery is a fundamental experience. One day, I finally saw how much I had received from all those sages who had given me a look, a smile, their consideration and their teachings. I asked myself, "What can I do for them? Give money to the ashram? Make a contribution to a Sufi *khanaqa*? That is so little. I cannot betray them by not being happy. It would be like turning up my nose at what they gave me and trampling their blessing underfoot . . . I am going to be happy out of love for them."

⁓ • ⁓

Learn, first, to fully appreciate what has been given to you. Keep your accounts fairly. "But if my child gets sick and . . ." For the time being, your child is in good health. Why write only what goes wrong on your inner account book and never what goes right? If I wake up one morning with a backache, I note that down. But if I wake up feeling fine, that is just natural; I do not feel particularly happy. I remember that it was during a stay at the ashram, when I was neither in very good form nor very happy, that Swamiji showed me how arbitrary this was. On awakening, I became fully aware that I had no aches or pains anywhere. If I were paralyzed and someone miraculously promised me that my legs would be perfectly normal again, how wonderful I would feel! There was nothing wrong with me physically . . . how wonderful! I was served a very Indian (but very good) breakfast – made up of green beans, vegetables and rice – and the river was there for me to wash in . . . how wonderful! I noted down what I had instead of what I did not have, and went on to note everything that came up: "The room is full of mosquitos and I have no more repellent" – "Yes, but I have a mosquito net for the night! . . ." This objective bookkeeping at Swamiji's ashram was a revelation for me: how could I be so happy when nothing new, nothing special had happened? Adopting an impartial view brings you closer to your natural state, which is plenitude. Why do you live with an impoverished heart? The simple fact that you are not suffering does not make you feel grateful. After three days I was so happy! Take a look at what you too have been given.

Do not refuse to be happy here and now, on the pretense that you were not happy in the past and you might no longer be happy tomorrow. If you are at a restaurant with someone you love, eating food you yourself have chosen and drinking your favorite wine, rejoice! Yes, it is true that the meal will not last forever, tomorrow you will be back at work again, but at least – now – be happy.

I do not like the word "duty" very much. Swamiji said, "*Man as man has no duty; man has only right and privilege.*" It is not a teacher's duty to teach, it is his or her right. It is not a doctor's duty to take care of the sick, it is his or her right. Still, I would like to use the word "duty" just now: it is your sacred duty to be happy. Not being happy is betrayal, it is blasphemy. I am not blaming you, but what is wrong? Keep better accounts of all life gives you. If you do, you will find yourself filled with wonder even within the next few days. And afterwards, you must continue this impartial bookkeeping.

Do not greedily take what is given to you; welcome it with an open hand. Remember Master Eckhart's words, "You can enjoy all the good things life gives you if you know that you are ready to let them go immediately, and just as joyously, if necessary." For the time being, life has not taken back all it has offered you. Dare to want to be happy. This is not selfishness. Ask God, ask life, for what will make you happy . . . yet at the same time accept "but may Thy will be done." You have the right to desire things, to desire them so strongly that you attract them. "But may Thy will be done." All is grace, I will not forget that; to everything, I will say "yes."

Wanting happiness is both right and legitimate. "Oh no, I should only ask for divine happiness! That is really spiritual. I want nothing but God Himself." Forget the fact that, in the morality of your childhood days, austerity may have preached before all else through hood days, austerity may have preached before all else through statements like, "We are not here on earth to enjoy ourselves; we are here to do our duty, to do honest work." What would be completely out-of-place for an older man is perfectly right for a young man of twenty. It would look a little strange for a forty-year-old to push a little plastic lawnmower around all day, although it is perfectly natural for a two-year-old. It is right for a young girl to go out dancing in nightclubs. But some of you come from a family context where that sort of thing was not done.

If religion was combined with an overly-rigid form of education, you came to the conclusion that God expected only austerity from you. Not at all! What is a Father? One who wants to give his children what will make them happiest. It has nothing to do with spoiling them. It is just giving. "Dad, can I go skiing with my friends next week?" You may not have enough money for your son to go skiing for a week, but God . . . he has the entire universe, so can he not give you all you want? Dare to ask. It is true that there will also be suffering. You cannot avoid all suffering. The convex inevitably comes with the concave. There is no way to have only the concave side. But that is no reason not to enjoy what can make you happy.

The difference between happiness that lulls you to sleep and divine happiness lies in the feeling of gratitude. Demanding-love is not love. When a man tells a woman "I love you," if what he means is "I want to be loved by you and no other," it may be flattering for the woman herself but that kind of love is not worthy of the name. Do you see any other way to attain real love except through gratitude? It is beautiful to pray, "I want to love, to stop being a prisoner of my childishness and self-centeredness." But make this your prayer too, "I would like to feel gratitude." The foremost religious, mystical word is "thank you." As I said before, "thank you" is not used in India; each one must express his gratitude in his own way. It is said that a quarter of an hour before dying, Ramana Maharshi – fully conscious – told the one who served him, "The English have a word, 'thank you.' I will simply say, 'I am content.'" Even the last known words of this sublime sage were an expression of gratitude.

The Path of freedom is not only "doing one's duty," it is being happy and even enjoying oneself. There are obstacles for all of us: our education; bad physical, emotional and mental habits that maintain us in suffering; the unconscious conviction that as long as we suffer we have a chance to attract the love we hope for, because an unhappy child usually attracts his mother's love. If a little boy is happy, he plays alone in his room. But if he cries, his mother takes him into her arms, saying, "My little darling, what's wrong? Mom loves you very much! You know that, don't you?"

One more point. It applies primarily to suffering, but consider it also from the viewpoint of human happiness, for it is this latter that will lead you to God. When we suffer, we feel that we exist. We feel crushed, we are in pain . . . but along with our distress there is a certain feeling of being, a certain consciousness of being. How can I feel that I really exist when I am happy, instead of when I am suffering? If you want to progress, you must do away with preconceived ideas that stop you from blossoming. How can you "be" and "grow" in happiness? If you look closely, you will see. Yes, that's it – by being happy. Happiness is our sacred duty. Ask. Insistent prayers are granted. All spiritual masters agree on that. Look at what life has given you – even if it is a source of happiness that is still fragile. If you are able to appreciate the fact that water flows hot from your faucet, you will appreciate the joy of having a husband who is a good husband after all, and a little son who is very nice. Do not worry today about the fact that fate could take them away from you. To live in fear of losing them is not to respect God who gave them to you. Not only do you not even dare ask, but when God grants your prayers, you do not know how to receive what he gives you.

Now we can go one step further, into the very heart of the quest – the egoless state. The reason we resist happiness is because the ego is lost. And it is understandable. That ego you identify with, which keeps you in duality, is all you know. Your ego gives you the feeling that you exist. Hindu wisdom, on the other hand, offers us the egoless state. The ego dies if you are really happy. The sense of separate individuality (*ahamkar*) disappears when there is happiness and gratitude. The ego can only maintain itself by complaining, begging, demanding, fighting, remaining withdrawn and rehashing old problems. I have kept the most important point for the end, the ultimate reason behind all I have said so far: the ego refuses to be happy because it will disappear. It can only subsist if it is against something. The words "yes" or "thank you" express the opposite of selfishness. You will only reach the egoless state through happiness and gratitude. But the mind is so twisted that it comes to the conclusion that it is more selfish to be happy than to be unhappy. I could do a survey, asking: "What do you consider more selfish: being happy or suffering?" Those who have never seriously thought it over would answer, "being happy."

God will only reveal himself to you in the form of happiness. It may be the happiness of Saint Teresa of Carmel or Saint Francis of Assisi, both of whom were ill but radiant just before they died. This joy could spring from suffering – when suffering is accepted, it turns into bliss. Do not distort mystic texts. "God is love." How could God reveal Himself to you as suffering? God prepares the way with trials. He sends suffering as an emissary. But God Himself only comes to you in the form of happiness. Plenitude makes self-centeredness disappear; it brings about the death to oneself spoken of in spiritual teachings. To be happy is to die to oneself. This is the ultimate teaching. Hindu texts present sexual union as a very high form of human happiness. If this union is really fulfilling, it is suicide for the ego – at least momentarily. But there are thousands of ways of making love: looking after lepers, praying for the world, helping a neighbor in difficulty, giving money to charity . . .

THE JUMP INTO LIFE

The ego can only subsist on the basis of past sufferings and frustrations. It represents the past that continues on into the present. A little child has no ego, then the ego is formed, and the Sage finally no longer has an ego. *Ahamkar* only survives through the memory of suffering and the fear that suffering will return. If it is happy, it opens up. Opening up is always the opposite of the ego. Our fear of dying to ourself betrays our fear of discovering that we are happy at last. We are afraid we might feel, "I don't know what to struggle against anymore; I don't know what to resist . . ." Right now, do not ask yourself what you are jumping into; ask yourself what you want to jump out of. ". . . I can't stay in this apartment any more, the house is on fire! I hope the firefighters have spread out that net you jump into . . ." One thing is certain – I want to jump, to jump out of my old life, out of the narrow role I play, out of my prison. And what will you jump into? Happiness. Jumping into happiness is jumping out of the ego.

When all is said and done, what Swamiji's teachings come down to is freedom through happiness. And to reduce them to nothing but *lyings,* in which early childhood sufferings are re-experienced, is to understand Swamiji very badly indeed. "*To be free from the pain, one has to be the pain.*" This is true, so "yes" to suffering. On this basis, some have understood that: "The Way is suffering; the going has to be rough; since there is not enough suffering in life, one must also suffer in *lyings.*" What Swami Prajnanpad says is just the opposite, "*Be happy.*" In a previous book, I mentioned that at the end of my first stay at his ashram, I wanted Swamiji to give me a mantram or some expression that would sum up his teachings in one phrase. "*Swamiji will give it to you when you leave.*" The next morning, after an early breakfast, when I went to prostrate myself before Swamiji, he said, "*Be happy, Arnaud.*" Those were his first words: "*Be happy, Arnaud.*" Next words, a few years later: "*You don't know what happiness is, Arnaud.*" Now I know. Not only is it not bad to be happy, it is the only possible defeat for the mind. The mind is one and the same as what forbids you to be at ease. One day I told a woman, "For you, the mind is what stops you from throwing yourself into that man's arms and saying, 'I love you'."

I remember how I too struggled. I was brought up in the midst of misunderstood Evangelical concepts, such as, "Those who shamelessly enjoy themselves, have fun and seek pleasure are egoists." What I am asking of you is far more terrible than getting up to meditate every night at 1 a.m.; it is far more terrible because it is the death of the ego. What becomes of the ego when it can no longer complain, no longer suffer, no longer be "against". . . ?

How else can God's love reveal itself to you, other than by offering you happiness? It is so simple: forgive, welcome, receive and keep your inner accounts fairly. All those sufferings you went through during the times when you were so unhappy have served as a passageway to happiness. You have dived into your sufferings so that you would come out wiser. At the heart of fully-accepted suffering, you find happiness. It is blasphemy not to be happy. It is rising up against God. Being openly unhappy is actually better than displaying a false, fixed smile and wearing a mask. Do not be a caricature. But the religion that will free you is that of being happy to the greatest possible degree – and thereby a maximum of saintliness through a minimum of ego.

8

THE POSITIVE APPROACH

JUST this afternoon I received a visit from a man who does not reg-
ularly come to our ashram but wanted specifically to see me. Life
seems to have given this man everything. He has been showered
with all our civilization has to offer: honors in his law studies, a successful career as a lawyer, a happy marriage, children who have
been a source of great satisfaction. He must be about 65 years old
and what he came to tell me was that he had deeply loved his wife,
that their relationship had been the most important thing in his
life for twenty-five years, but that due to a surgical error, she had
died two years ago. "I can't get over it," he confided, "life has no
meaning for me any more. All I do is work myself into a stupor . . .
I feel I can't go on like this. Can you help me? I believe you're supposed to be a man of wisdom; perhaps you could give me some
advice." What advice could I give him, other than, "Dedicate yourself now totally to the most important thing of all – the spiritual
quest."

What struck me was that, although this was a man who had had
access to all kinds of information and had surely received some
religious instruction in his youth, the essence itself of spirituality
seemed non-existent for him. He had heard of monks, of Buddhists,
of Hindus . . . But apart from that, the very reality that can be read
in the eyes of Ramana Maharshi or a Tibetan master, the strong
testimony of the words of a sage or sacred scriptures, that to which
thousands of beings of our own times – in monasteries in Bhutan,
Sikkim, Japan, India or the Western world – devote their time and

energy . . . none of that meant anything to him. I tried using words like 'wisdom', 'spirituality', 'mysticism' – they did not get through to him. I was talking about a reality that did not strike any chord in him. Still, he had come to see me.

And I wondered, "What radical difference is there between this man whose wife's death has dealt him his own 'deathblow' – a man who, though highly cultured, is ignorant of all that is called spirituality – and those who have heard of Karlfried von Dürckheim, Krishnamurti, Ma Anandamayi, Ramdas or Milarepa? Are those who claim to draw their inspiration from spirituality really so convinced that everything they experience gives them an opportunity to progress, that everything is a blessing – or, like this man, do they lack faith under it all? Is the difference as obvious, for example, as that between a blind man and a man with normal vision?" For my visitor, his bereavement was nothing short of a disaster. It was purely and simply a cruel blow of fate. What was the difference between his approach and the one (be it Oriental or Christian) which had gradually become part of me, an approach affirming that everything, always, has meaning? Remember the promise I myself have so often quoted, "Everything works toward the good of those who love God."

I could easily imagine what one of the masters I had approached in the past or an advanced disciple on the path would have said, not in a vain attempt to console him, but with total conviction: "But there is meaning to your bereavement! You must not see it as a tragedy! It is a beginning, it is a blessing, it is a transition . . ." Orientals go even further. They say that if he and his wife had truly loved each other (and he said this was so), her greatest act of love for him would have been to leave him, even if she had not consciously decided to die . . . for in the fathomlessness of destinies, in the fathomlessness of the affinities between people's personal pasts, the greatest proof of her love for him would have been to go, because only her death could have brought about an awakening in him, a drastic change that would become the starting point of a new life. And, of all I said, this was perhaps the only thing that got through to him, ". . . if it has not profoundly changed your life, then she has died for nothing! The way to show real faithfulness to your wife is not to be overwhelmed with grief and fall to pieces but to progress, to go even further toward your own fulfillment!" What I was saying seemed outrageous to him; nonetheless I felt that it struck a responsive chord.

I can still hear Swamiji's words, "*a fully positive approach to life.*" This always has something to do with faith, even for someone who is not religious and does not speak in religious terms. You know how strong a role faith plays in the Gospels as well as in various mystical paths that still inspire people today. Ramdas' entire works, starting with the description of his own personal search, entitled *In Quest of God*, are a superb illustration of this. Faith like this is a certainty: it is being certain of the meaning you give your life; it is the conviction that each event, each situation in which you find yourself, always has positive value – even a staggering blow, even tragedy, even a bolt of lightning from a cloudless sky. When a perfectly healthy seventeen-year-old is killed in a mountaineering accident, can his mother see that as the divine guru at work, as God's love at work?

In their despair over a death, people often turned to sages who had reached a high level of radiance. When they went to Ma Anandamayi, her answer was always, "It is a blessing from God! It was your child's karma to make you experience the ordeal of his own death because this hardship is necessary for you to find the supreme Good, beyond birth and death." Spiritual teachings do not deal only with ordinary human realities, they refer above all to the supra-human level or, if you prefer, to the fully human one. (For me, they are synonymous.) Spiritual teachings are not just a factor of improvement, giving positive effects within the ordinary framework of one's life. In other words, they cannot be reduced to forms of psychotherapy – even very refined ones – since they incite us to turn immediately from the psychological to the spiritual.

It is because spiritual reality exists, because you can experience it personally and your experience can be confirmed by the testimony of all the sages of history, that our hope is not an empty daydream or a comforting illusion, but a "conviction of unseen realities" as the New Testament describes faith. You who have discovered spiritual teachings, can you take this positive approach? Everything is based on it. Those who were deeply wounded at the very beginning of their lives have a pessimistic view of life. But isn't it paradoxical if, once they discover spirituality, they keep their negative approach year in and year out?

Swamiji told me that if a child had really felt wanted and loved at the beginning of his life, even if he later underwent shocks, deep down inside he would keep a positive approach. But if that had not been the case and he was scarred too early by strong trauma before he really had the chance to feel love, he would have a painful perception of life. Moreso than others, someone who has a negative approach to reality feels that "life is suffering," "life is pain," while one who was loved by his mother in early childhood but lost that love – or thought he lost it – holds the deep-down conviction that happiness exists and that life has meaning, even if there are voices in him that say, "Happiness will never again be mine." In moments of despair, he feels "Light exists, beauty exists, perfection exists, but unfortunately I have no right to it all; I seem to have been branded by fate."

One who has a negative approach to life sees life itself as absurd, disastrous. But he or she may discover the spiritual dimension and come to the conclusion that there reigns another reality, a luminous one, beyond this desolate life. In other words, life has no value, apart from the look in Ma Anandamayi and Ramana Maharshi's eyes; these latter have gone "beyond the beyond of the beyond" as the Mahayana Buddhist *Prajnaparamita* says. But within us is a purely and absolutely positive life force and that remains forever unaltered. There are *vasanas* in us, there is interest in this manifested world, there is a sex drive – even if it is repressed, inhibited and twisted. Therefore, those who do not believe in this life, but who do believe in Buddha or Jesus Christ's sainthood and who would like to spare themselves simple existential happiness, are not all qualified to open up immediately to the light of the Self and to discover, within a few years, a transcendence within which all is bliss.

Some who are engaged in the spiritual search willingly believe that sages have attained perfection but that they themselves cannot directly realize the absolute because they still have numerous ordinary demands in life. For example, a woman may want to be a mother and to experience life with a partner and, at the same time, be convinced that marriage can never be a success, because of childhood, or even past-life, trauma. These desires, which cannot be denied, are expressions or deflections of the fundamental life force that makes birds sing, trees grow, winds blow and volcanos spit fire. And for man, this fundamental life force reveals itself in the form of thoughts, sensations, emotions, sexual urges, cultural and artistic interests and various ambitions.

These drives are there; your attraction for spirituality will not let you deny them. However all of life in the relative – which makes up our path until we become established in the Ultimate – is experienced by some of you in a negative manner: "You bring children into the world and they turn against you; no gratitude. You get married and, before long, your husband starts looking at other women . . ." In contrast, one who has the inner certainty that life has meaning tends to believe in happiness, even if at times he is disappointed. He is convinced that there can be a beautiful relationship between a man and a woman, between parents and children; he is sure that communication with others, the feeling one gets from nature, art, all aspects of life, are sources of great joy. Life fills him with wonder even if it sometimes seems harsh.

Swamiji was right in saying that it is very difficult for those with a positive outlook to relative existence to understand those who have a negative outlook to it. Why does he get discouraged so quickly? How is it that he doesn't believe in anything? Why is he or she always so sad and bitter, with such a disillusioned attitude? "Things always go wrong, I told you so!" Obviously, if we have such an outlook, each divorce reinforces our attitude . . . "I told you there was no such thing as love between a man and a woman." Each time a child appears somewhat ungrateful to his parents . . . "I told you a mother's life was nothing but sacrifice. She never gets anything in return." When we think that way, everything ends up feeding and reinforcing our negative outlook.

⌒ · ⌒

My understanding of faith could be summed up in one sentence: faith is a positive approach to life. Someone who has faith cannot but have a positive approach to life. Sages make a clear distinction between "faith" and "belief" – and they know what they are talking about. Beliefs, which are based on dogma, are usually a source of misunderstanding and even conflict between the different religious traditions. For example, Christians believe in the Trinity which is an abomination to Moslems. Faith, however, cannot divide men because it emanates from another kind of reality: a reality which is *one*.

What are known as the three theological virtues are three stable, deep feelings: faith, hope and charity. Faith is the conviction that unseen realities exist, the certainty that light, indestructible life and God's grace are constantly at play. In its wake comes hope. "Hope" is to be distinguished from "hopes". For the latter, "things'll work out tomorrow when . . . or if . . . or if and when . . ." Hope has to do with the spiritual dimension of life: "I'll manage, I'll reach the goal, there's a divine, transcendent meaning to life. It's no longer possible for me to despair." And charity – or love – leads to living in love like a fish lives in water and so, of course, to feeling loved. These are three aspects of the same inner realization.

Why love? Because if you have faith and hope, and therefore this positive approach, you will feel that the world, reality, life, is not fundamentally hostile to you – as some believe. You will be unable to feel that it would have been better never to have been born into a reality which is an enormous nightmare (as some philosophers have gone out of their way to describe it) or that the world is "absurd." On the contrary, you know that life loves you. Remember what Chandra Swami said to a woman here: "The Divine or Nature is not cruel at all. It is very, very compassionate, more compassionate than a mother." It must be said that in India, as a rule, a mother is a real mother, the embodiment of love.

If you have faith and hope, your life is illuminated by love. God loves me, Life loves me . . . even at the very moment when my son is dying, when I learn that I have cancer, when my firm is liquidated, when the woman I trust completely falls in love with another man . . . This is where there should be a radical difference between one who is committed to a spiritual path and one who is not.

These last fourteen years of opening up to others have brought me face to face with a reality that confirms Swamiji's words: it is possible to be receptive to spirituality and yet to retain a hopeless vision of life. There is something there that must be seen and transcended. As long as this negative approach dominates your life, you are not on the Way. Perhaps you are preparing yourself to be one day fully committed to the Way, after a long period of purification through suffering. Perhaps you will then make very rapid progress. But you cannot consider yourself on the Way until you are prompted by faith, a firm personal belief, hope and love. You will only be able to love if you feel that life loves you, or eventually that your guru or God himself loves you. I can readily say that universal energy, the source of the manifestation, loves you. Can you imagine an ocean that does not love the waves through which it expresses itself? That would be a contradiction in itself. How can one recognize spiritual truth and at the same time remain negative? How can you be committed to a spiritual path and still have neither faith nor hope nor the feeling that life is love? Paradoxical though it may seem, that is nevertheless the case for many who consider themselves sincerely committed to the Way.

Some feel that they are reborn when they come upon books that bear witness to spirituality. Even if I have been very unhappy, life suddenly takes on new meaning. I discover Ramana Maharshi, Ramdas, Ma Anandamayi, Djalal ud-din Rumi; I know that wisdom and saintliness exist. I hear of the *atman,* of Buddha Nature; I am moved by sacred scriptures and works of art. Teachings still exist… I will search; I will find a master. As of that moment, one can no longer fall into total despair. But the really beautiful thing is to see someone, whose approach has always been negative, awaken one day to a positive approach and believe that Christ's or Buddha's promises apply to him, even if he still leads a very unassertive and frustrating life. Up until then, his negative approach stopped him from blossoming but grace acted in him, hope was born, and with it came a new inner attitude that little by little will change his life.

One day someone asked me, "How can I progress in spite of everyday difficulties?" I gave the somewhat hard answer, "How can you get up to the second floor in spite of the stairs?" If you are on the first floor, to a certain extent the steps themselves separate you from the second floor, but at the same time they are what will bring you up there. So the real question on the path is: "How can I progress on the Way *thanks* to everyday difficulties?"

In opening up to that dignified man, seeing how powerless I was as he told me that life had lost all interest for him since the sudden death of his wife two years earlier, I felt that for someone with faith, the ordeal in which this man found himself would be purely positive. It would open up a new stage in his life, maybe the richest of all, the most precious, one that would enable him to surpass what had certainly been a fulfilled human life – but within human limits – and to reach transcendent life. To go back once more to an image that is so well-known but so true: the caterpillar must disappear for the butterfly to be born. The butterfly knows a dimension that the caterpillar does not – the third dimension of space; instead of sliding along leaves, he flies. This is a perfect illustration of the metamorphosis awaiting you.

When will those who do not believe in life be given the oppor-tunity to have a positive attitude? What I can say – and it is the most precious and most important thing you can hear if you are one of those who retain a negative approach alongside true spiritual aspi-ration – is that it has been given to me to see several people, who were walled up in their negativity, one day go through a total change. What a blessing! This change is required of those in whom the con-viction that the supreme value is love, not suffering, has not yet crystallized. If it has happened once, it can happen twice or ten times . . . and why not for you? This is the first line of hope.

The second hope is based on an intellectual understanding – because although someone despairs of life, intellectually he can be quite lucid and be a good technician or a good scientific researcher. The life force itself remains unaltered in everyone. So even if the negative mark is very close to the source, underneath your despair or your lack of faith, you remain unscathed. No one is destroyed at the source – ever – it is impossible. Life can con-tradict itself, it can divide into opposite forces struggling against each other, but at the origin it is *one,* and this non-dual life goes on animating us. Even in the form of despair, it is this same force that is expressing itself.

Indeed, no matter how mutilated you are, you can be sure that, deep within, you remain unaffected. You have only to rediscover the consciousness you knew before the moment when the wound became engraved in you. Just as the wicked fairy curses the infant on his christening day in fairy tales, even if you prove to me that this curse comes from past life *samskaras* when you died amid tor-ture and betrayal, I will still say to you, "The life force is unim-paired." Whether or not the problem comes from far back in your past in no way alters the fact that reality is purely positive. In every being, *brahman* proclaims: "*Aham brahmasmi*", "I am the absolute, the infinite, immensity." Eventually, some hear it. When this intel-lectual approach convinces you, it can turn into feeling and bring about an inner change. But it is not the only approach.

Even without entering into the subtleties of Christian theology or the Hindu *bhakti* path, all the manifested forms of what can be called grace cannot be denied. Whatever testifies to this faith, this hope and this love can have a beneficial influence on us, for example, the *darshan* (meeting) of sages, a look that strikes you in a photograph, a certain style of architecture, *satsang* (the coming together of people who share the same quality of appreciation for spiritual values). It is a coming together to reinforce one's faith. If you have the opportunity to take part in Tibetan rites where the intensity is heightened by the presence of a master, or to take part in offices in a monastery that continues to attract spiritual seekers, then a little of that faith, that hope and that love is deposited in you.

According to Indian tradition – and I now have proof that it is true – everything not only has material reality but also fine materiality (*sukshma*). In saying that a little of this faith is deposited in you, what I mean is that just as you incorporate the food you eat, you also assimilate a subtle reality. This is why it is said in India, "*Sarvam anam,*" "everything is food": *satsang*, singing *kirtans*, rites such as *pujas*. You receive these influences – it is as if you just have to open your mouth and food is put into it. And by virtue of being deposited in you, this materiality ends up saturating and crystallizing. The amount of time it takes varies – sometimes more, sometimes less. The faith shown by others, their hope and their conviction that life is love, are instilled in you little by little. You remain wounded and hurt, "I don't believe it, it isn't for me, I'll never manage," and then one fine day, the crystallization completes itself and there is an inner conversion. This is another line of hope.

You probably acknowledge the existence of a reality of another order, a reality that the lawyer I mentioned earlier has never heard of, a reality of which he has no inkling. But I must dare to be firm and you must face the truth: as long as you keep a negative approach, you cannot truly progress. This may seem like a cruel thing to say, but in reality it is not because there is a cure. The most important thing is to be cured. Do not remain engulfed in your sadness. Some Westerners I knew had spent years in India and nonetheless continued criticizing everything. Things always went wrong for them. They were bitter; they found their lot cruel and unfair; they were convinced that nothing was right in the world. Even if you adhere to metaphysical doctrines which state that the relative world is transitory and that there is no reality other than the "light of perception" or the "witness" (*sakshin*), the fact is that your entire life takes place in the relative world. Your first step must therefore be to reconcile yourself with this world.

There is a contradiction that you must become keenly aware of and it is this: on the one hand, believing that ultimate reality (*satchidananda*: being, consciousness, bliss) expresses itself through the world of opposites and, on the other, considering that this world is nothing but suffering and despair. If all is *brahman*, if the world of dualities is the manifestation of oneness and light (as the Gospel of Saint John says), and if in theory you adhere to this reality, do not contradict yourself. Why do you come here? Even if you were not deeply moved by Ma Anandamayi or Ramana Maharshi, some dynamism obviously oriented you in this direction. It remains to be seen whether you are living in total contradiction with the driving force of this dynamism or if you trust it.

Obviously, what I say is always based on personal convictions which I am trying to share with you. Those who deny spiritual reality are convinced that there is no proof of what I maintain. Yet I join a multitude of others and affirm in my own turn that this is not an assumption but rather an experience. Now, those who have borne witness were either speaking of something they knew nothing about (they completely fabricated it all and there is no reason for you to believe them) or, on the contrary, they were relating their own personal experience . . . like Ramana Maharshi, whose consciousness rejoined the ultimate, like the *rishis* – the great visionaries of the Upanishads – and especially like Christ, who took on the title "Son of man." The early Church insisted on the human nature of Christ: "God became man so that man could become God." All men have this divine inner nature, just as Christ took on our human nature. People are often shocked – and then moved – when I remind them that the son of God squatted to shit. Otherwise Christianity loses all meaning. It is because the early Church insisted so strongly on Jesus' humanity and Christ's divinity (to the point of being cruel and unjust toward heretics), that the Orthodox Church has always insisted on man's "deification," that is, man's vocation to actualize his divine nature.

This is promised to all of you, both by early Christianity and by the Upanishads which say: "You too are That." Everyone knows of this phrase, but everyone may not know of the dialogue between Svetaketu and his father. That famous phrase comes from a passage which compares man's potentialities with those found in a simple piece of fruit: hidden within the fruit lies a small seed; if this seed sprouts, it will become a tree and that tree, in turn, will bear fruit with new seeds able to produce other trees, and so on. So powerful is the life force that, within a few years, just one blade of grass would cover the entire earth if there were no destructive force to oppose its expansion. Saying "You are That" is another way of affirming man's divine nature and his potential to become God.

If your heart understands this phrase, "Everything works toward the good of those who love God," and if you are sure that it applies to you, you have found the road to salvation. However, your unconscious is laden with *vasanas,* desires and drives that have been more or less accepted or smothered by education and trauma. So you find yourself in the position where you want to receive from the relative world. And this is normal. It takes a long time to be able to place all one's hope in the absolute. Like you, I was not immediately able to aspire exclusively to fusion with God or to the encounter with the "Supreme Friend," as Sufis say. You must consider the demands within you – from the more gross ones (I want to be admired, I want to be recognized, I want to be told that

I am better than others) to the much finer ones (I would like to experience a real love relationship with a woman or a man, I would like my children to be happy and fulfilled, I would like what I write to be beautiful and moving, I would like to sail around the world . . . whatever). Everyone has his own list.

This world of human aspirations, which cannot be side-stepped, is linked not only to your search for spiritual perfection but also to a fundamental inner state of dejection that declares, "It doesn't work; I'll never achieve it." And the primary characteristic of a negative approach is to grasp hold of all that reinforces one's pessimistic view of the world and to override whatever could put it into question. In other words, it is a tendency to see only the signs and facts that confirm your pessimism and to ignore those that contradict it.

This year, at the European Union of Yoga Federations in Zinal, Switzerland, a Hindu Swami was asked a question. His name is Swami Satchidananda and he is a true representative of India now living in the United States. Swami Satchidananda answered, "You do not see all that life has given you; you only see what it has not given you." Although this is a common function of the mind, it is none the less striking. In the same way, not a moment goes by without your seeing what is wrong – but not what is right. A father has two children: one is a source of pure joy to him, the other is difficult. He only talks to me about the difficult child, never about the happy and smiling one. Is that right? The mechanisms are sometimes that simple and that obvious.

What is a negative approach to life? When we first hear the word "negative," it carries a certain background emotional coloring for us – it evokes a pessimistic, bitter, disillusioned attitude. But all it means is negation, the attempt to deny. Why do we speak of a negative approach to life? What does it deny? This approach is, of course, the concrete negation of the ultimate values that we may otherwise approve, philosophically speaking. It is the negation, in acts, of our spiritual convictions. But it is also the denial of reality as it is; it is my refusal to see what I do not want to see; it is my refusal of what would contradict my attachment to hopelessness.

～‥つ

Now let me go a little further. I cannot immediately prove what I am saying to you, like a physics teacher who carries out an experiment in front of his students. Still, I swear that what the dualistic tradition says about God's grace at work (or miracles) is true. I swear to you that if you "Seek first the Kingdom of God and His justice . . ." then "all else . . ." – that is, all that is really necessary for you to find the Kingdom of God – "will likewise be given to you." On one occasion when I cited this extract from the Gospels, a woman let out the heartfelt cry, "Even a lover?" – "Yes!" Naturally, a priest cannot say that. "Yes!" I cannot promise that you will win the Nobel prize for literature if you are a novelist, but I can assure you that you will receive what is really necessary for you, what you want above all else, as long as you want it with both insistence and perseverance. On countless occasions I have seen proof of Swamiji's teachings (which were expressed in scientific terms rather than religious ones) concerning the "law of attraction." It works in the same way as a magnet attracts a pin.

If you had faith, you would see. It is just that it takes years before you can believe this. Or perhaps you put a little faith in it, but when what you want is not immediately given to you, you get discouraged. These words, coming from a man who for a long time floundered about in his own contradictions, may strike a chord in you – because I too am a Westerner. If first (not "exclusively" but "first"), you seek the Kingdom of God and His justice . . . light, truth, boundless life . . . you will see that life is full of love and that God is love. A Reality that corresponds to what we call "God" does indeed exist – it is not just a consolation for the weak or an invention of theologians. And you will discover that this Reality is, as Chandra Swami said, "so loving, so compassionate." You are steeped in an ocean of love but you do not feel it. When I stayed at Ramdas' ashram, I caught a glimpse of that, but soon after leaving I forgot it. The law of attraction does exist. Some who had had a particularly hard and difficult life did not let themselves become discouraged and they received what the Gospel calls "the crown of glory." All traditions emphasize how important it is not to become discouraged. And one day, if you persist in your quest without ever losing hope, the miracle happens.

There is something you can do to bring about this positive approach when you are on the Path: do not simply look at what life has not given you; look at what it has given you. First of all, it has given you what is most precious of all. The man I saw today, full of dignity and generosity toward others, has not yet received this most beautiful of all gifts. It is the belief that Christ and Buddha were right, the knowledge that Ramana Maharshi, Ma Anandamayi and Ramdas walked this earth in the twentieth century and that the tremendous world of supreme spirituality is a reality that concerns us all. Life has given you the most beautiful gift of all. Feel that. Be grateful to life and be grateful to yourself for having attracted such a gift. Think of that lawyer with nothing but his distress because his wife has died. His despair is meaningless: "I am a broken man, there is no reason for me to live anymore." You have sensed an eternal reality, that of Christ, Djalal-ud-din-Rumi and Ramana Maharshi. As Swamiji said, thank yourself. I have been capable of attracting this gift! You have discovered a world of which some know nothing: they leaf through a book on Buddhism but do not buy it; they find that a divinely serene statue of Buddha lacks a bit of expression: "A Picasso is more forceful." Ah, your heart should be full of gratitude! You have been showered with more than Dustin Hoffman and Robert Redford combined, more than Reagan and Kennedy combined. It is true – otherwise, why would you be reading a book like this?

Life is love for everyone. It cannot be otherwise. One day you will discover that this is not just a nice-sounding – but empty – phrase. To go back to an image mentioned before which I have always found very meaningful: can the ocean deny even one of its waves? Can the ocean wish harm on even one of its waves? The ocean itself is in each wave and each wave is in the ocean. An ocean of faith, hope and love expresses itself in you, holds you, supports you and surrounds you. Divine reality is in you and you are bathing in divine reality. But as we know, man has lost awareness of his origin. Ignorance, blindness or original sin has exiled man (the word "Adam" simply means "man") from the perfection, the paradise, that he must find anew.

Life can offer you new opportunities – provided that you are able to welcome them. If you maintain a negative attitude, you prevent great accomplishments from coming to you. If you dare to take the first step, little by little everything will change. Everything will not change immediately and miraculously, giving you nothing but success in all domains. Certain great joys may even turn into trials. After searching for so long, you could meet the man of your dreams, the one you have been waiting for; you could be wonderfully happy together . . . and he could die four years later. But from light to light, from truth to truth, you ascend toward the Kingdom of Heaven, toward that perfection which alone can fulfill you. Perhaps you will experience trials, but on another level – allowing you to progress and giving you inner wealth and maturity. You cannot know exactly what life will bring you in the relative but each time a discouraged, mediocre human being, at odds with himself, dares to take the first step, life responds. This first step will sometimes be asked of you at the very moment when you have lost everything . . . .You find a master, an excellent yoga teacher or a very good psychotherapist and he suddenly dies in an accident . . . or your husband abandons you for another woman . . . or you lose your job . . . or you have financial problems that look like they will never be solved . . . And if you are then capable of saying a real "yes" to your destiny, at that very instant you open the door to the path in whose name so much will be given to you. Even if one day you must endure great suffering, it will make you grow and bring you toward ever more light.

I can tell you that among those who have been practicing this path for a long time, as well as among the "new generation" (those who have recently met Arnaud in person for the first time), a few have started this process of self-transformation and their destiny has changed. The law of attraction has acted in their favor; they no longer view life in the same way and instead of speaking in a sad and disillusioned way, they have a constructive attitude. They have finally stopped going round in circles. Their lives are no longer a constant repetition of the same failures. But a reversal of attitude is always at the root of these changes. Everything is based on that. When will you have sufficiently heard, seen and recognized the truth of what I am saying to dare take the first step and personally turn your negative approach into a positive one? To a certain extent, it depends on you. Each time life becomes difficult again, all your hope rests in yourself: will you take the first step and say a whole-hearted "yes" to life?

"There is no love in my life." I can understand this cry from the heart. A child may not have been loved by his mother, or he may have been loved less than his little sister. Naturally, since he felt unloved – even if his family was a normal one – he did not blossom. He therefore became less lovable; he was liked less than others by his teachers at school and by the other children . . . Once this process is under way, it goes on repeating itself. Suffering attracts suffering. A southern French proverb says, "Stones go into heaps." These "heaps" are actually large piles of stones that were gathered from the fields so that farmers could cultivate the "garrigue" (scrubland). Swamiji also quoted an English proverb for me that owes nothing to Hindu wisdom: "*Nothing succeeds like success; nothing fails like failure.*" If you start to succeed, you gain confidence, you become positive and you attract more success. If you start to fail, you get discouraged, you become negative, you attract failure again . . . all of which proves to you that your disillusioned attitude is justified, that life will never give you anything and that you are right to expect nothing.

Even if you have never studied alchemy, you probably know of the alchemical principle: one needs gold to make gold. To change lead into gold, an alchemist must start off with some gold. This idea is also found in the Gospels: "Every one who has, shall receive; but from him who has not, even that which he has shall be taken from him." There must be (I say "must" because it is a law) a little positive seed in you, a little gold, if you want to change the lead of life into the gold of blessing and spiritual life.

If you dare to take the first step and say "yes, yes" – you are saved. A woman one day confided to me, "There is no love in my life, I have never been loved." And she added, "Never has a man told me 'I love you' – never – not even as a lie or without meaning it." I remember answering, "Well then, love something. Do you like these flowers?," "Oh yes," she said, "they are really beautiful!" – "Then love them." Love, and I promise you that things will change.

"I promise you." How bold it is to declare that the simple fact of loving can change everything! Some of you in this room today, or others who will later read these words, will say that it is not true: "I have been suffering for ten, fifteen years now, and Arnaud has been promising me that things will get better, that I mustn't get discouraged, that light is promised to all and therefore to me, and I can see that it is not true. What worked for Arnaud, what worked for others, will never work for me." Did you really take the first step? Or did you make a false attempt, just to be able to say that you tried and to show me that I was wrong? That is the real issue. You cannot cheat with the spiritual.

Decide to love. Just do it – love. Take the first step. Everything is based on love. Success in your job comes from feeling that life loves you, that your bosses, your directors and your colleagues are not your enemies. Success in politics comes from feeling that life loves you because it brings you to power and voters love you. Success in the artistic field, becoming a Louis Armstrong or a Jacques Brel, comes from feeling that life loves you, that the public loves you and loves what you do. Everything comes down to love.

Not long ago, I heard a very revealing remark from a woman who comes to Font d'Isiere. There were several of us in an Asian restaurant, looking at a painting of a Chinese woman stretched out on the ground with her hand under her chin, and everyone was giving a different interpretation of the painting. But it was this woman's interpretation that struck me most: "It is a woman in bad straits because she has no man in her life." That is heartrending. The woman who pronounced those words suffered that very situation for a long time. But her fate changed – because she changed.

So it is all a question of love. A positive approach to life means this: for me, nature or the divine is compassion. And a negative approach implies: for me, life (and to say "life" is to say "the divine" or "nature") is not love. Chandra Swami, who embodies the wisdom that has come to us from India, gave this answer to a person I know well and in whom I have taken much interest. For years this woman has done nothing but cry out her suffering. When she asks to see me, it is to talk about the despair she feels without my really being able to get through to her. When she writes to me, it is once more to speak of her suffering, and it is this same suffering that she expressed to Chandra Swami, saying "I suffer so much I'm afraid I'll go crazy." And the Swami answered her: "The divine or nature is so compassionate." His is the positive approach to life: "The divine or nature – and I add life – is love." And the negative approach persists in crying out: "No, no, you don't have the right to say that, Arnaud! You cannot have suffered, if you dare say that life is love. Life is not love, otherwise it would not relentlessly torture me."

Of course I can understand your rebelliousness. But it is nonetheless true that all spiritual beings have shown that it is possible to adopt a luminous approach in the very heart of what others consider to be suffering. The end of Saint Francis of Assisi's life was an example of this. Those close to him saw him racked by a very painful illness. But when a disciple one day ventured to say: "For a great servant of God, God is very hard on you!," Saint Francis cried out: "How dare you say that! Do you for one instant doubt God's love?" This is the meaning behind the sometimes misunderstood words: "The sufferings of a saint sing God's glory." The eternal Father is not a sadist who takes delight in his servants' sufferings. The sufferings of a saint sing God's glory because a saint's quality of radiance amid disaster bears testimony to the supernatural. All those who have approached a suffering saint, who have seen him or her subjected to great trials, would agree on this, whatever the saint's religion may be.

Before Bernard Benson and Frederic Leboyer came to his aid, Kangyur Rinpoche lived in poverty. One of his sons had tuberculosis and Kangyur Rinpoche was unable to have him treated; rain came through the roof of the sort of attic that served as a home for his family. Meeting that man, who had been thrown out of Tibet and was living in utter destitution, drastically changed not only my existence but also that of Bernard Benson. This latter was a man who had met Nixon and many other celebrities and had turned himself from an English engineer into an American millionaire within a few years. "I've met the most powerful men in the world," he confided, "but when I saw Kangyur Rinpoche, I saw a Man for the first time in my life."

Love is everywhere but, for the time being, do not tremble with fear, thinking: "I want nothing to do with a love that is going to come to me as persecution! I don't want love that reveals itself in the form of sufferings, like what Ramana Maharshi or Saint Francis of Assisi went through, even if they were both radiant saints." Don't take it like that; instead, remember Chandra Swami's words: "Life is love." To be positive is to dare to listen to such a statement, even if you do not yet have proof of it. Actually, you do have some proof: you have discovered the spiritual world – and that is the greatest gift life could have given you. You are alive; you have an undamaged brain with which to listen; your lungs are in good breathing condition; you have a capacity of awareness enabling you to feel energy and life within yourself. What more can you ask for? Well? It is up to you to say "yes."

Even if your wounds are deep, I beg you to listen to me. I like the way Buddha put it: "Oh! disciples, out of love for yourselves, I beg of you . . ." – as if Buddha were humbly imploring his disciples! Will you do something out of love for yourself? Out of love for yourself, I beg of you, look closely at what I am explaining today. Why are you negative? Why does your attitude say "no" to what you otherwise recognize as true? The very fact that you are listening to me or reading this proves that you do recognize it. Why this "no"? "No, life is not love. No, the words of sages and the promises of Christ are not true! No, what Swamiji said does not apply to me." Yes, they are true. Take the first step. In this world of love, decide to love! And you will see!

~··~

I have just referred to two Hindu Swamis other than Swamiji and their words have been illuminating. How are you going to rediscover the hope they offer you? How are you going to stop being negative? Simply say "yes." Swamiji's entire teachings are contained in the English word "yes" – a word that became a true mantram for me. And as you know, to say "yes" is first of all to say "*it is.*" To what are you going to say "*it is*"? Before all else, start by eliminating "*it is not.*" Swamiji was very strict on that point. With "it is not" and "I don't have," nothing is possible. "I don't have a husband, I don't have a good child who is a bright student, I don't have a faithful wife, I don't have an interesting job . . ." With what is not and what you are not, you are at a standstill. No progress is possible. What can you do with what is not? Do you want to cross a pond in a boat that does not exist? Do you want to kill an animal with a gun that does not exist? I can tell you that during the nine years I knew him, Swamiji very often cut me short on this: "What are you saying Arnaud? You are negative again; you are talking about what is not, what you don't have, what you are not able to do – only unreality." To become positive is to stop constantly bringing into your life what you are not and what you don't have.

Second point in becoming positive: never again consider that what you have not had up until now, you will never have and what you have not been up until now, you will never be. At least that much. If you have never had money up until now, do not make a decree implying: "I'll never have money. I'll never even once have enough to take a trip." Naturally, if you have a European physique, you will never look like a Senegalese. But apart from these obvious facts, many changes that you do not even suspect can come about. Don't ever make the mistake of projecting onto the future. "*Up until now* I have not had" – that is all. Catch yourself red-handed at these inaccuracies, like "I who never have any money" – as if it were understood once and for all that you never will. From now on, require yourself to think in this rigorous way. *It is.* And you will see what is. If you rely on the support of what is, you are on solid ground and you can move forward.

Third point: see what is fortunate. It is not a case of daydreaming or of vain consolations; it is a case of pure realism. If you are not paralyzed or obliged to walk with a cane, be aware of that. I have already told you of the discovery I made in that area, one day at Swamiji's ashram. He had just attracted my attention to the mind's characteristic of keeping inner accounts by noting down only the things that make us suffer. This does not concern intense sufferings, like losing a son, but rather all the little refusals that make up our day. If one day the hot water heater breaks down and the water is ice-cold just as I am ready to step into the bathtub, I note it down immediately. But I do not ordinarily notice that I have hot water to wash with every morning. When Swamiji emphasized that simple reality, I spent my next three days at the ashram really becoming aware of all the fortunate things in my life. At the end of those three days, although nothing had changed and I had not received any fantastic news from France, I was so happy I almost couldn't bear it! I wondered at being able to see and to walk, at having enough to eat, a bed to sleep in and those light clothes worn in India so as not to suffer from the heat. Being positive consists in no longer counting up what you do not have and instead, in recognizing what you do have.

And finally, the last point: being positive means using what, today, you consider to be suffering, as a starting point, without forgetting hope and faith. It means daring to believe that life loves you at the very moment it seems to be betraying you: yes, my wife has a lover; yes, for now I am alone and haven't found the companion I am looking for; yes, repeated attempts to get an interesting job have failed and I'm now doing something that has nothing to do with what I want. . . If you say "yes" to these painful aspects, you will see that, within them, they carry the promise of a greater joy. It is true. I realize that for you today these words are still only a matter of faith, that is, your conviction of what is as yet invisible. But if you manage to say a wholehearted "yes," a positive "yes" to *what is* in difficult circumstances, you will have proof that life is not unrewarding.

One day, one of the participants of the ashram came and told me:

– "Arnaud, I wasn't able to get much schooling when I was a boy; I was a teenage dropout; I have no real abilities. As you know, I've always thought that I was made for better things and I want nothing to do with little mediocre jobs. But for the time being, I haven't accomplished anything important. I don't want to live in a dreamworld any more – I am what I am. Ever since you asked me to take the first step, I've been doing it. I've been saying "yes." I can at least do that.

– "And just what are you going to do, on a practical level?"

– "Well, I'm going to ask for a government job pushing papers in a Public Health office. I'd like to be in contact with the public, even if it only means being yelled at, behind one of those counters . . . any old mediocre job. For the time being, I'm dropping my lofty ideas." Off he went to the Public Health headquarters in the city of Nimes to file an application. Two months later, even though he had no diplomas, a friend offered him a job requiring an engineering degree! He took the job; he did well and he who had accepted to earn one thousand dollars a month started earning almost three thousand soon afterwards. That is a true story! And it is not the only one; I could tell you others.

YES, yes – this is the most positive word of all, the magic word. Say "yes" to your life; you will see the miracles that ensue. If you are on the path of truth, you will immediately plug into a deep current with which you are not usually in contact and attract new opportunities. It doesn't only happen to others. I am well-aware that even if I cite the examples of one or another among you who has adopted this positive attitude and who has seen the miracle come about, you will answer: "Yes . . . for them but not for me!" But that is not true, it is the same law for everyone – and thus, also for you.

I am saying this to you because seeing that man who represents some of the elite of our modern society gave me a very intense feeling; he has benefited from all the intellectual and cultural values this latter has to offer and yet he has not even caught a glimpse of what is called spiritual reality. You have. For now, accept this dimension of life with confidence. Some have been completely lost and no longer are today. I used to be lost myself; I no longer am. When I was young, I waited a long time for life to bring me a stroke of luck; yet it always seemed to be a day away. I even wrote a sort of romanticized-version of life in a sanatorium, although it did not interest any publisher. My inspiration came largely from patients I met there, but of course all the protagonists of my story revealed different aspects of myself. I recently read a passage where I had written: "He hung onto those words: 'the darkest hour is just before dawn,' but the darkest hour was always followed by an even darker hour and dawn never came." At the age of twenty-seven, those were the words I put into the mouth of one of my characters. Obviously, they betrayed a projection of a part of myself. Even if I was able to write such a seemingly desperate passage, Swamiji considered that my approach to life was totally positive. It is true that deep inside I was sure that light, truth and love existed.

~ ∙ ∙ ~

Even if you have not yet received from life, change your attitude. Become positive. You can do something about that. Others have done it, so you can too. But persevere. Impatience does you a great deal of harm. If I had told any of those who came to the Bost [*the first ashram set up by Arnaud and Denise Desjardins*] in the beginning, "It will take you at least six years to begin to understand anything of these teachings," they would have found it unbearable. Most came with frustrations on the one hand and a certain feverishness on the other, asking for quick results because they had been suffering for too long. Each came with his own problems from which he or she wanted to be free as quickly as possible. Those to whom I tried to tell the truth did not want to hear it, "Oh no, for me things must go quickly, I'll put on a spurt if necessary." They did not go quickly, they did not put on a spurt and the six years went by . . . Meanwhile, the few steps that they could have taken along the way during those six years – but which they considered derisive and beneath them – were never taken.

"*You cannot jump,*" Swamiji used to say. It is true that you can walk quickly instead of dawdling along. But if it takes you two years to get past one stage and you consider that too long, I am afraid that six years later you will have accomplished nothing at all. Impatience is disastrous for spiritual seekers. All traditions say so. If you are impatient, at fifty-five you will find yourself at more or less the same stage . . . trying to lie to yourself, to hide your failure and to fool and dope yourself with self-illusion. This will lead to nothing but an ever-increasing state of ill-being. And you will always put off a definitive cure for your suffering until tomorrow. I even heard these terrible words from the mouths of people who had consecrated their lives to Gurdjieff or Krishnamurti: "Me, I won't make it in this life; the die is cast." Indeed, I heard them from the mouth of a man who has his own disciples.

Several times, Swamiji told me the story about the two yogis meditating on the banks of the Narmada . . . They are doing their penances and spiritual exercises and along comes the god Brahma. The first yogi asks, "O Brahma, when will I be free?" Brahma shows him a coconut tree with several very large leaves on it, saying "Do you see how many leaves there are on that tree? That is the number of lives you still have to live before you will be free." And the yogi is shattered: six, eight, perhaps ten leaves when what he had wanted to know was whether he had six months left or two years. The other yogi then bows and says, "O Brahma." But notice the subtle difference; he does not ask the question in exactly the same manner. Instead of asking, "When will I be free?," he inquires "Will I be free one day?" Brahma tells him, "You see that tree?" He points to a tulsi tree – a very common tree in India, with tiny leaves as numerous as the hairs on a man's head. "Well you see, you will be free after you have been reborn as many times as there are leaves on that tree." And all the yogi hears are the words: "You will be free." And he cries out in wonder, "I will be free!" Then Swamiji concluded, "*and at once he is free,*" because he went beyond time. If you can accept – and accept with your whole being – that you have a thousand lives yet to live, the ego will vanish and you will be free at that very moment. For the time being, just hear these words "One day, I will be free."

Do not be impatient. Instead, consider yourself engaged in a great undertaking. Those same Westerners – so convinced that they will do better than Tibetans, and that it will take them three months to do what Tibetans do in twelve years – do not hesitate to agree that it takes ten years to become a specialized doctor, that it takes years of dance rehearsal or piano practice to become a virtuoso, and that it takes a lot of work to get through advanced math classes and engineering school. But in the spiritual domain, they imagine that, being Westerners, they have the privilege of going faster than others. The Way has often been compared to climbing a mountain, on top of which all mountaineers meet. Back in 1964, before he left Darjeeling, a Tibetan master by the name of Kalu Rinpoche met a few of the rare Europeans who were highly enthusiastic about Tibetan Buddhism. Through an interpreter, he told me, "Westerners all believe that the answer is to be dropped off by helicopter on top of the mountain, although it is fine for all those naive Tibetans to climb up on foot, carrying their knapsacks. You will never get there." As Swamiji said, "*There is no short cut.*" Nothing says you have to dawdle along the way or drop into every bar along the road. And there is certainly nothing that says you must read all the signs wrong and drive straight onto the motorway in the direction of Paris when you want to go to Rome. Do not turn your back on the truth and then moan over the fact that it takes a long time. If you do exactly the opposite each time you have a chance to put the teachings into practice, you may well destroy the few worthwhile and admirable efforts you have made elsewhere.

I was once present when Swami Ramdas told someone, "You are digging a hole with one hand and putting the earth back into it with the other." That will never get you anywhere. Many seekers do just that, even though they go out of their way in other respects. For example, they may take the trouble to get up at six in the morning to meditate or they might give up enjoyable holidays to die of heat in an Indian ashram during the month of July. But then they counteract such moments of courage and determination by doing exactly what defeats their purpose during the rest of their lives.

Before deciding whether you can make the journey in a Chevrolet or a Jaguar, first make sure that you are on the right road and going in the right direction – even if you are on foot. If you walk twenty miles a day, you can cover quite a distance, you can get as far as Fatima or Jerusalem. Alexandra David-Neel, a woman of the twentieth century, actually walked from China to India, by way of Lhassa. Walk two years, three years, five years . . . and if you get a little closer to the goal every day, you will reach the goal. But it is not a matter for mere amateurs. Go to the same trouble as a young man who has decided to be a racing cyclist does. He will pedal two hours every morning before work, day after day, as he dreams of becoming the yellow jersey who will lead the Tour de France. Apply yourself. And for the time being, forget what you have heard about non-effort, about giving up all effort and about direct spontaneity; it is all true – but it is not something that you can immediately apply.

⌣·⌣

The price that must be paid is actually two-fold. On the one hand, there are daily, perhaps hourly, efforts to put into practice what you are convinced is right and necessary on the path you are following. You receive explanations. You are shown how emotion functions and how your mind creates an unreal, constantly frustrating world. What is said is explained and proven; you are not required to have blind faith. Certain attitudes that call for almost permanent awareness are suggested to you so that you can catch yourself red-handed in untruth and come back to the reality of *what is*. To attain metaphysical non-duality, you must practice non-duality in daily life. This means no longer personally creating duality between what you consider as "me," and what you consider as "other-than-me" (whoever or whatever this "other" may be), and by being "one with."

The second aspect is both delicate and difficult to explain. So please listen without emotion because it is your cure or non-cure that is at stake. A certain amount of boldness is necessary in life. Swamiji often told us: "*Be bold.*" You cannot lead a frightened, petit-bourgeois life. Traditionally, the seeker of truth has been compared to a dauntless hero who ventures off the beaten path, a knight braving monsters and dragons. There is nothing ordinary in abandoning all the satisfactions this world has to offer in order to become a hermit in a cave; there is nothing ordinary in renouncing all the pleasures of our consumer society in order to become a Carthusian or Trappist monk. It is not your vocation to live in a monastery, but I must admit that I am surprised to see how many of you try to reconcile a narrow existence with the search for the truth.

In the name of the Fatherland and the Resistance – which is a less elevated cause that that of God – some have taken enormous risks. They have hidden arms in their houses, become affiliated with networks and ventured back and forth across Paris after curfew. Many died – shot, gassed or cremated; others were tortured by the Gestapo. Numerous men and women from all over Europe exposed themselves to countless dangers instead of sleeping peacefully in their beds at night. Can a spiritual seeker not also take risks? If you look around you, it is obvious that there are some people who have always led very restricted lives, while others have shown boldness. I remember learning in history class about Bernard Palissy who burned all his furniture in order to discover the secret of ceramic enamel. Who among you is ready to burn his or her furniture to seek the truth? Apart from our daily practice of the teachings, there are moments when spiritual destiny knocks at our door – and it is important to know how to seize the opportunity when it arises.

No matter how spiritually ill you are, if you thirst for a cure, you will have this boldness. I have known invalids who have done everything possible to recover from an incurable illness, going so far as to have themselves taken by stretcher to Padre Pio and then to Lourdes. Are you capable of that kind of determination to obtain the spiritual cure that we are talking about today? You may have heard the expression, "God vomits the lukewarm from his mouth." It is so true. A certain kind of folly in the eyes of men is wisdom in the eyes of God – not only in the ultimate sense of the word but in the way we live our own lives.

I am going to speak of my own experience once more, so as not to use only Milarepa or Tibetans as examples. Looking back now, I realize that each time I had a choice to make, I always opted for what I felt and understood to be spirituality – in relation to whatever level I was on at the time. Oh, that level certainly did include much weakness and childishness as well as many false ideas; it also sometimes led me to make mistakes and go astray. There were constant financial worries in my job due to the fact that, although I was under contract, I was paid fees instead of a fixed salary. Yet every time I managed to put a few pennies aside, so to speak, I went back to India at my own expense (whenever I was not being sent there by the television company) to obtain precious help from Ramdas, Ma Anandamayi or Kangyur Rinpoche. And I am surprised to see how many of those I meet lack this kind of boldness. I am not talking about reckless behavior, such as something an eighteen-year-old boy might do and pay very dearly later on. I am talking about a boldness that comes from deep within, a boldness that corresponds to the feeling that people used to have when they said, "God wills it." I have no doubt that my wife Denise and I behaved for years in a way that was folly in the eyes of men. When I worked in television, it was folly to turn down important programs where I could have been first assistant to a great director, so as not to miss even one evening of the sacred movements and dances that we practiced in the Gurdjieff groups. It was folly to travel from Paris to India on untarred roads, under the conditions in which we left in 1962 – without money and with a four-year-old daughter – and then again in 1964, when we took along a three-and-a-half month old baby. It was nonetheless a reasonable folly, considering that I had the name of a French-speaking pediatrician every three or four hundred miles along the road. Wherever there was a Turk, an Iranian or an Afghan who had studied medicine in France, I had managed to get the address. When he was four-and-a-half months old, the baby was in Ma Anandamayi's arms; when he was six months old, he was in the Dalai Lama's arms. God wills it – off we go. As it turned out, the children came back in perfect health, even though they had been sick once or twice. Such was our faith that, "God wills it," they got better.

A risk taken can also turn out badly. Some heroes of the Resistance were shot. If the intensity of your spiritual search drives you to take certain actions or to behave in a certain way, I cannot promise you that, materially, it will bring about nothing but advantages . . . like shooting interesting films which can later be made into good programs. Where can you find positive influences? You must give without being sure to receive. No petty calculations, like "I won't go and see that Tibetan rinpoche unless I'm sure I'll receive a great blessing." If there is a chance, I will go. If nothing happens and if it is a failure, I have no regrets; I tried.

I am not saying that you should all quit your jobs tomorrow and take off to India for six months. Everyone's case is different, of course. But you cannot live a protected life without ever running any risks and at the same time be a spiritual adventurer. Be bold. Be mad in your own way; have that folly in the eyes of men which is wisdom in the eyes of God. Take risks; seek, seek again, seek everywhere, seek in every manner, do not miss any opportunity or any possibility that fate gives you. And do not be mean and stingy by trying to bargain the price.

Give with all your heart and you will receive. Do not let opportunities escape you. One of you recently told me, "I feel that there is no time to lose. I still have much to receive from India – but will India always be there?" No. Who would have believed, when I was filming in Afghanistan in 1973, that two years later, those same Sufis would be persecuted and shot and that their villages would be napalmed? India still holds treasures today; it has more to offer than just a few famous sages surrounded by thousands of Westerners. Yet with nothing more than a change of political regime, foreigners could be restricted to traveling in tour groups; individual visas might no longer be granted. And then it would be too late. We always wake up when it is too late . . . "Ah, if only I had known!" But it takes more than regrets to make up a *sadhana*. If, in your life, you retain a nostalgia for all that your lack of courage kept you from doing, you will not grow older feeling: "I did what I had to do; I received what I had to receive; I gave what I had to give."

I have had some contact with members of the Explorers Society.

What boldness they show for expeditions that are in no way spiritual! They may go to the heart of the Amazon, where they will be stung by mosquitos and bitten by snakes . . . or set themselves adrift on a boat, like Alain Bombard, where they run the risk of sinking a hundred times over, just to prove that it is possible to live on plankton and seawater. And you, with your spiritual motives, you want to take things cautiously and be sure of the results in advance. The years go by. You are twenty-five . . . thirty-five . . . then suddenly you realize that you are forty and your first white hairs begin to appear. Don't wait until it is too late and then start regretting things. Put the teachings into practice every moment if possible . . . or every hour, if you cannot do it every moment . . . or once a day, if that is the best you can do. And seek out all that can help you.

Looking back to when I was young, I can see myself totally immersed in a certain childishness and gullibility but, at the same time, burning with a fascination for spirituality and deeply stirred by the books I read on the subject. Although at first glance I had no possibility whatsoever of going to India, I remembered hearing once, in the Gurdjieff groups, that Mont-Saint-Michel was a truly "objective" work of art, whose architecture conveyed the laws of spirituality. I set off for Mont-Saint-Michel as if I were going to meet God. It is no great feat to go to Mont-Saint-Michel, but I felt "I have an appointment with God at Mont-Saint-Michel." My imagination and my inner projections undoubtedly played a great part; I even ended up disappointed because I had expected too much. And then I read that the church at Vezelay was also a sacred work of art – a mecca of spiritual vibrations – so off I went to Vezelay. It was not a very difficult trip for a Parisian, but I remember the feeling I had when I took to the road; it was that same feeling that later led me to Bhutan, to Sikkim and to Japan.

To each his own destiny. Do not imitate; do not copy. You are not meant to shoot films for television. But one thing is categorically true: you will get nowhere on the Way unless you put in the effort. It would be dishonest of me to help you merely cradle your dreams.

But leave here with this good news deep in your heart: it is possible to be cured. I promise that to all of you. And I would like to say those words while looking straight into the eyes of some I know who are even more lost than others. There are some who feel powerless in the face of their anguish, their neuroses and their inability to conduct their own lives – but even to them, I can solemnly promise that a cure is possible. There is a path; there is a way; there is a method. Buddha taught it. Christ also taught it and although the language he used has been distorted, that does not make it any the less true. Swamiji, an unknown Bengali guru, also pointed out the Path. Muster up a tiny bit of imagination and picture this: me – not Ramdas – me; me – free; me – completely at ease in life; me – fulfilled. That sounds just as unbearable as: "It'll take you twenty years." Yet it is true. And if you have the crazy audacity to go beyond time – like the yogi who accepted to be reborn as many times as there are leaves on a tulsi tree – perhaps your awakening will take place sooner than you and I can predict just now.

BRIEF GLOSSARY
of Sanskrit terms used by Arnaud

ahamkara: the ego, awareness of oneself as a separate individual; "I am me" (separate from others).

ananda: bliss, peace, happiness; Self-awareness.

anandamayakosha: one of the coverings of the self, the covering of personal bliss.

Atmashakti (shakti): the great force of universal life; energy.

Atman: the Supreme Self, the supra-personal state, the Absolute.

aum (om): amen, yes, acceptance; sacred syllable, symbol of Brahman.

Brahman: the Ultimate, the Absolute.

bhakti: devotion.

bhoga: the conscious fulfillment of acknowledged desires; true appreciation, real experience.

chakras: the subtle energy centers of the body.

chitta: the psychism (a person's entire unconscious, the depository of all his or her memories - both conscious and unconscious); the storehouse of all one's samskaras , i.e. all the latent tendencies which one carries engraved within oneself.

chitta shuddhi: purification of the psychism.

darshan: sight (seeing a sage, a divinity).

darshana: way of seeing something, angle of vision.

dvandas: pairs of opposites

gopis: shepherdesses in love with Krishna.

hara: Japanese word for the center of gravity in the lower abdomen.

hridaya: the heart.

karana sharir: the causal body.

karma: action. The law of cause and effect. The totality of a person's actions including the consequences of those actions. Personal destiny.

kirtan: devotional song or singing.

klesha: a spot or stain.

koshas: coverings of the Self:

- physical
- physiological
- mental or emotional (psychological)
- objective intelligence
- personal bliss

kundalini: very powerful energy at the base of the spine.

lingam: a phallus; famous verticle black stone sculpture; symbol of Shiva.

lying: (English word with no corresponding Sanskrit term)
Technique developed by Swami Prajnanpad for the purification of the unconscious; a plunge into one's unconscious in
order to consciously live out unconscious trauma.

maithuna: the sex act, mating.

manas: the mind, as the basis of egocentric thought and false
perception of reality. (At times, one's entire psychological
manner of functioning.)

manonasha: destruction of the mind.

maya: the unreality of the world, illusion.

moha: attachment.

prana: subtle energy contained in the air and in foods,
accumulated through conscious breathing.

pranayama: mastery of energy through breathing techniques.

prajna: wisdom, understanding.

prarabdhakarma: karma that will inevitably bear fruit, whether
or not one attains Enlightenment.

pratyahara: taking away the objects of the senses; yogic
internalization.

psychism: (not a Sanskrit term; word used as equivalent of
French "psychisme"); see chitta.

puja: Hindu rite.

rajasic: active.

rishis: the great seers or visionaries of the Upanishads.

sadhana: the path, the way, spiritual discipline, conscious effort in view of Liberation.

samadhi: ecstasy, supra-individual consciousness, being "one" with all.

samskaras: subconscious latencies or tendencies, the weight of the past, deep impressions proper to each individual.

satchidananda: being-awareness-bliss; Buddha nature, the Self.

satsang: the company of spiritual seekers.

satvic: calm, serene, internalized.

Shakti (atmashakti): the female principle; energy; fundamental or divine energy; the unique and infinite energy revealed through all deaths and births. Cosmic energy.

sharir: body.

shastras: Hindu moral laws (like the ten Commandments).

Shiva: the male principle; the witness, the immutable. God of destruction and death; the Benevolent.

shunyata: Emptiness, the belief in the emptiness and unreality of all phenomena.

sukshma sharir: the subtle body.

sthula: the "gross" level of Manifestation (as opposed to the causal and subtle levels).

upa-bhoga: ordinary happiness; indulgence; false, impulsive, mechanical appreciation of things; the more or less unconscious fulfillment of desires which are not fully recognized; (experience which does not help one to progress along the spiritual path).

Upanishads: Hindu texts of wisdom.

vasanas: needs, unsatisfied demands, fears, desires, latent tendencies (to redo, relive and re-experience what has already been done, lived and experienced).

vasanakshaya: eroding away one's vasanas.

vijnanamayakosha: one of the coverings of the self, the covering of objective intelligence.

vrittis: great or small disturbances of the psychism.

yoni: a cup; the female sex organ; the supporting cup-like base of the lingam.